Henry James OM (15 April 1843 – 28 February 1916) was an American-British author regarded as a key transitional figure between literary realism and literary modernism, and is considered by many to be among the greatest novelists in the English language. He was the son of Henry James Sr. and the brother of renowned philosopher and psychologist William James and diarist Alice James.

He is best known for a number of novels dealing with the social and marital interplay between émigré Americans, English people, and continental Europeans. Examples of such novels include The Portrait of a Lady, The Ambassadors, and The Wings of the Dove. His later works were increasingly experimental. In describing the internal states of mind and social dynamics of his characters, James often made use of a style in which ambiguous or contradictory motives and impressions were overlaid or juxtaposed in the discussion of a character's psyche.(Source: Wikipedia)

Literary works:
Watch and Ward (1871)
Roderick Hudson (1875)
The American (1877)
The Europeans (1878)
Confidence (1879)
Washington Square (1880)
The Portrait of a Lady (1881)
The Bostonians (1886)
The Princess Casamassima (1886)
The Reverberator (1888)
The Tragic Muse (1890)
The Other House (1896)
The Spoils of Poynton (1897)
What Maisie Knew (1897)

PICTURE
AND
TEXT

HENRY JAMES

PRINCE CLASSICS

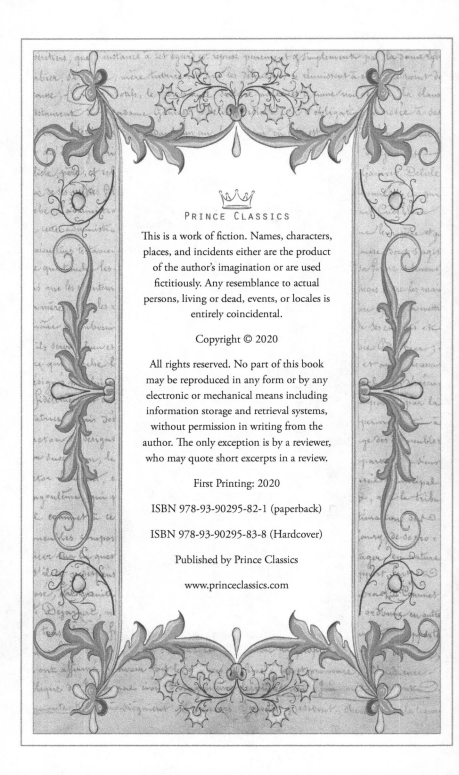

PRINCE CLASSICS

First Printing: 2020

ISBN 978-93-90295-82-1 (paperback)

ISBN 978-93-90295-83-8 (Hardcover)

Published by Prince Classics

www.princeclassics.com

Contents

PICTURE
AND
TEXT

NOTE

Two of the following papers were originally published, with illustrations, in Harper's Magazine and the title of one of them—the first of titles has been altered from "Our Artists in Europe." The other, the article on Mr. Sargent, was accompanied by reproductions of several of his portraits. The notice of Mr. Abbey and that of Mr. Reinhart appeared in Harper's Weekly. That of Mr. Alfred Parsons figured as an introduction to the catalogue of an exhibition of his pictures. The sketch of Daumier was first contributed to *The Century*, and "After the Play" to *The New Review*.

BLACK AND WHITE

If there be nothing new under the sun there are some things a good deal less old than others. The illustration of books, and even more of magazines, may be said to have been born in our time, so far as variety and abundance are the signs of it; or born, at any rate, the comprehensive, ingenious, sympathetic spirit in which we conceive and practise it.

If the centuries are ever arraigned at some bar of justice to answer in regard to what they have given, of good or of bad, to humanity, our interesting age (which certainly is not open to the charge of having stood with its hands in its pockets) might perhaps do worse than put forth the plea of having contributed a fresh interest in "black and white." The claim may now be made with the more confidence from the very evident circumstance that this interest is far from exhausted. These pages are an excellent place for such an assumption. In Harper they have again and again, as it were, illustrated the illustration, and they constitute for the artist a series of invitations, provocations and opportunities. They may be referred to without arrogance in support of the contention that the limits of this large movement, with all its new and rare refinement, are not yet in sight.

I

It is on the contrary the constant extension that is visible, with the attendant circumstances of multiplied experiment and intensified research— circumstances that lately pressed once more on the attention of the writer of these remarks on his finding himself in the particular spot which history will perhaps associate most with the charming revival. A very old English village, lying among its meadows and hedges, in the very heart of the country, in a hollow of the green hills of Worcestershire, is responsible directly and indirectly for some of the most beautiful work in black and white with which I am at liberty to concern myself here; in other words, for much of the work of Mr. Abbey and Mr. Alfred Parsons. I do not mean that Broadway has told these gentlemen all they know (the name, from which the American reader has to brush away an incongruous association, may as well be written first as last); for Mr. Parsons, in particular, who knows everything that can be known about English fields and flowers, would have good reason to insist that the measure of his large landscape art is a large experience. I only suggest that if one loves Broadway and is familiar with it, and if a part of that predilection is that one has seen Mr. Abbey and Mr. Parsons at work there, the pleasant confusion takes place of itself; one's affection for the wide, long, grass-bordered vista of brownish gray cottages, thatched, latticed, mottled, mended, ivied, immemorial, grows with the sense of its having ministered to other minds and transferred itself to other recipients; just as the beauty of many a bit in many a drawing of the artists I have mentioned is enhanced by the sense, or at any rate by the desire, of recognition. Broadway and much of the land about it are in short the perfection of the old English rural tradition, and if they do not underlie all the combinations by which (in their pictorial accompaniments to rediscovered ballads, their vignettes to story or sonnet) these particular talents touch us almost to tears, we feel at least that they *would* have sufficed: they cover the scale.

In regard, however, to the implications and explications of this perfection of a village, primarily and to be just, Broadway is, more than any one else. Mr.

Frank Millet. Mr. Laurence Hutton discovered but Mr. Millet appropriated it: its sweetness was wasted until he began to distil and bottle it. He disinterred the treasure, and with impetuous liberality made us sharers in his fortune. His own work, moreover, betrays him, as well as the gratitude of participants, as I could easily prove if it did not perversely happen that he has commemorated most of his impressions in color. That excludes them from the small space here at my command; otherwise I could testify to the identity of old nooks and old objects, those that constitute both out-of-door and in-door furniture.

In such places as Broadway, and it is part of the charm of them to American eyes, the sky looks down on almost as many "things" as the ceiling, and "things" are the joy of the illustrator. Furnished apartments are useful to the artist, but a furnished country is still more to his purpose. A ripe midland English region is a museum of accessories and specimens, and is sure, under any circumstances, to contain the article wanted. This is the great recommendation of Broadway; everything in it is convertible. Even the passing visitor finds himself becoming so; the place has so much character that it rubs off on him, and if in an old garden—an old garden with old gates and old walls and old summer-houses—he lies down on the old grass (on an immemorial rug, no doubt), it is ten to one but that he will be converted. The little oblong sheaves of blank paper with elastic straps are fluttering all over the place. There is portraiture in the air and composition in the very accidents. Everything is a subject or an effect, a "bit" or a good thing. It is always some kind of day; if it be not one kind it is another. The garden walls, the mossy roofs, the open doorways and brown interiors, the old-fashioned flowers, the bushes in figures, the geese on the green, the patches, the jumbles, the glimpses, the color, the surface, the general complexion of things, have all a value, a reference and an application. If they are a matter of appreciation, that is why the gray-brown houses are perhaps more brown than gray, and more yellow than either. They are various things in turn, according to lights and days and needs. It is a question of color (all consciousness at Broadway is that), but the irresponsible profane are not called upon to settle the tint.

It is delicious to be at Broadway and to *be* one of the irresponsible profane—not to have to draw. The single street is in the grand style, sloping slowly upward to the base of the hills for a mile, but you may enjoy it without a carking care as to how to "render" the perspective. Everything is stone except the general greenness—a charming smooth local stone, which looks as if it had been meant for great constructions and appears even in dry weather to have been washed and varnished by the rain. Half-way up the road, in the widest place, where the coaches used to turn (there were many of old, but the traffic of Broadway was blown to pieces by steam, though the destroyer has not come nearer than half a dozen miles), a great gabled mansion, which was once a manor or a house of state, and is now a rambling inn, stands looking at a detached swinging sign which is almost as big as itself—a very grand sign, the "arms" of an old family, on the top of a very tall post. You will find something very like the place among Mr. Abbey's delightful illustrations to, "She Stoops to Conquer." When the September day grows dim and some of the windows glow, you may look out, if you like, for Tony Lumpkin's red coat

in the doorway or imagine Miss Hardcastle's quilted petticoat on the stair.

II

It is characteristic of Mr. Frank Millet's checkered career, with opposites so much mingled in it, that such work as he has done for Harper should have had as little in common as possible with midland English scenery. He has been less a producer in black and white than a promoter and, as I may say, a protector of such production in others; but none the less the back volumes of Harper testify to the activity of his pencil as well as to the variety of his interests. There was a time when he drew little else but Cossacks and Orientals, and drew them as one who had good cause to be vivid. Of the young generation he was the first to know the Russian plastically, especially the Russian soldier, and he had paid heavily for his acquaintance. During the Russo-Turkish war he was correspondent in the field (with the victors) of the New York *Herald* and the London *Daily News*—a capacity in which he made many out-of-the-way, many precious, observations. He has seen strange countries—the East and the South and the West and the North—and practised many arts. To the London *Graphic*, in 1877 he sent striking sketches from the East, as well as capital prose to the journals I have mentioned. He has always been as capable of writing a text for his own sketches as of making sketches for the text of others. He has made pictures without words and words without pictures. He has written some very clever ghost-stories, and drawn and painted some very immediate realities. He has lately given himself up to these latter objects, and discovered that they have mysteries more absorbing than any others. I find in Harper, in 1885. "A Wild-goose Chase" through North Germany and Denmark, in which both pencil and pen are Mr. Millet's, and both show the natural and the trained observer.

He knows the art-schools of the Continent, the studios of Paris, the "dodges" of Antwerp, the subjects, the models of Venice, and has had much æsthetic as well as much personal experience. He has draped and distributed Greek plays at Harvard, as well as ridden over Balkans to post pressing letters, and given publicity to English villages in which susceptible Americans may get the strongest sensations with the least trouble to themselves. If the trouble in each case will have been largely his, this is but congruous with the fact that he has not only found time to have a great deal of history himself, but has suffered himself to be converted by others into an element—beneficent I should call it if discretion did not forbid me—of *their* history. Springing from a very old New England stock, he has found the practice of art a wonderful antidote, in his own language, "for belated Puritanism." He is very modern, in the sense of having tried many things and availed himself of all of the facilities of his time; but especially on this ground of having fought out for himself the battle of the Puritan habit and the æsthetic experiment. His experiment was admirably successful from the moment that the Puritan levity was forced to consent to its becoming a serious one. In other words, if Mr. Millet is artistically interesting to-day (and to the author of these remarks he is highly so), it is because he is a striking example of what the typical American quality can achieve.

He began by having an excellent pencil, because as a thoroughly practical man he could not possibly have had a weak one. But nothing is more remunerative to follow than the stages by which "faculty" in general (which is what I mean by the characteristic American quality) has become the particular faculty; so that if in the artist's present work one recognizes—recognizes even fondly—the national handiness, it is as handiness regenerate and transfigured. The American adaptiveness has become a Dutch finish. The only criticism I have to make is of the preordained paucity of Mr. Millet's drawings; for my mission is not to speak of his work in oils, every year more important (as was indicated by the brilliant interior with figures that greeted the spectator in so friendly a fashion on the threshold of the Royal Academy exhibition of 1888), nor to say that it is illustration too—illustration of any old-fashioned song or story that hums in the brain or haunts the memory—nor even to hint that the admirable rendering of the charming old objects with which it deals (among which I include the human face and figure in dresses unfolded from the lavender of the past), the old surfaces and tones, the stuffs and textures, the old mahogany and silver and brass—the old sentiment too, and the old picture-making vision—are in the direct tradition of Terburg and De Hoogh and Metzu.

16

III

There is no paucity about Mr. Abbey as a virtuoso in black and white, and if one thing more than another sets the seal upon the quality of his work, it is the rare abundance in which it is produced. It is not a frequent thing to find combinations infinite as well as exquisite. Mr. Abbey has so many ideas, and the gates of composition have been opened so wide to him, that we cultivate his company with a mixture of confidence and excitement. The readers of Harper have had for years a great deal of it, and they will easily recognize the feeling I allude to—the expectation of familiarity in variety. The beautiful art and taste, the admirable execution, strike the hour with the same note; but the figure, the scene, is ever a fresh conception. Never was ripe skill less mechanical, and never was the faculty of perpetual evocation less addicted to prudent economies. Mr. Abbey never saves for the next picture, yet the next picture will be as expensive as the last. His whole career has been open to the readers of Harper, so that what they may enjoy on any particular occasion is not only the talent, but a kind of affectionate sense of the history of the talent, That history is, from the beginning, in these pages, and it is one of the most interesting and instructive, just as the talent is one of the richest and the most sympathetic in the art-annals of our generation. I may as well frankly declare that I have such a taste for Mr. Abbey's work that I cannot affect a judicial tone about it. Criticism is appreciation or it is nothing, and an intelligence of the matter in hand is recorded more substantially in a single positive sign of such appreciation than in a volume of sapient objections for objection's sake—the cheapest of all literary commodities. Silence is the perfection of disapproval, and it has the great merit of leaving the value of speech, when the moment comes for it, unimpaired.

Accordingly it is important to translate as adequately as possible the positive side of Mr. Abbey's activity. None to-day is more charming, and none helps us more to take the large, joyous, observant, various view of the business of art. He has enlarged the idea of illustration, and he plays with it in a hundred spontaneous, ingenious ways. "Truth and poetry" is the motto legibly stamped upon his pencil-case, for if he has on the one side a singular sense of the familiar, salient, importunate facts of life, on the other they reproduce themselves in his mind in a delightfully qualifying medium. It is this medium that the fond observer must especially envy Mr. Abbey, and that a literary observer will envy him most of all.

Such a hapless personage, who may have spent hours in trying to produce something of the same result by sadly different means, will measure the difference between the roundabout, faint descriptive tokens of respectable prose and the immediate projection of the figure by the pencil. A charming story-teller indeed he would be who should write as Mr. Abbey draws. However, what is style for one art is style for other, so blessed is the fraternity that binds them together, and the worker in words may take a lesson from the picture-maker of "She Stoops to Conquer." It is true that what the verbal artist would like to do would be to find out the secret of the pictorial, to drink at the same fountain. Mr. Abbey is essentially one of those who would tell us if he could, and conduct us to the magic spring; but here he is in the nature of the case helpless, for the happy *ambiente* as the Italians call it, in which his creations move is exactly the thing, as I take it, that he can least give an account of. It is a matter of genius and imagination—one of those things that a man determines for himself as little as he determines the color of his eyes. How, for instance, can Mr. Abbey explain the manner in which he directly *observes* figures, scenes, places, that exist only in the fairy-land of his fancy? For the peculiar sign of his talent is surely this observation in the remote. It brings the remote near to us, but such a complicated journey as it must first have had to make! Remote in time (in differing degrees), remote in place, remote in feeling, in habit, and in their ambient air, are the images that spring from his pencil, and yet all so vividly, so minutely, so consistently seen! Where does he see them, where does he find them, how does he catch them, and in what language does he delightfully converse with them? In what mystic recesses of space does the revelation descend upon him?

The questions flow from the beguiled but puzzled admirer, and their tenor sufficiently expresses the claim I make for the admirable artist when I say that his truth is interfused with poetry. He spurns the literal and yet superabounds in the characteristic, and if he makes the strange familiar he makes the familiar just strange enough to be distinguished. Everything is so human, so humorous and so caught in the act, so buttoned and petticoated and gartered, that it might be round the corner; and so it is—but the corner is the corner of another world. In that other world Mr. Abbey went forth to dwell in extreme youth, as I need scarcely be at pains to remind those who have followed him in Harper. It is not important here to give a catalogue of his contributions to that journal: turn to the back volumes and you will meet him at every step. Every one remembers his young, tentative, prelusive illustrations to Herrick, in which there are the prettiest glimpses, guesses and foreknowledge of the effects he was to make completely his own. The Herrick was done mainly, if I mistake not, before he had been to England, and it remains, in the light of this fact, a singularly touching as well as a singularly promising performance. The eye of sense in such a case had to be to a rare extent the mind's eye, and this convertibility of the two organs has persisted.

From the first and always that other world and that qualifying medium in which I have said that the human spectacle goes on for Mr. Abbey have been a county of old England which is not to be found in any geography, though it borders, as I have hinted, on the Worcestershire Broadway. Few artistic phenomena are more curious than the congenital acquaintance of this perverse young Philadelphian with that mysterious locality. It is there that he finds them all—the nooks, the corners, the people, the clothes, the arbors and gardens and teahouses, the queer courts of old inns, the sun-warmed angles of old parapets. I ought to have mentioned for completeness, in addition to his pictures to Goldsmith and to the scraps of homely British song (this latter class has contained some of his most exquisite work), his delicate drawing's for Mr. William Black's *Judith Shakespeare*. And in relation to that distinguished name—I don't mean Mr. Black's—it is a comfort, if I may be allowed the expression, to know that (as, to the best of my belief, I violate no confidence in saying) he is even now engaged in the great work of illustrating the comedies. He is busy with "The Merchant of Venice;" he is up to his neck in studies, in rehearsals. Here again, while in prevision I admire the result, what I can least refrain from expressing is a sort of envy of the process, knowing what it is with Mr. Abbey and what explorations of the delightful it entails—arduous, indefatigable, till the end seems almost smothered in the means (such material complications they engender), but making one's daily task a thing of beauty and honor and beneficence.

IV

Even if Mr. Alfred Parsons were not a masterly contributor to the pages of Harper, it would still be almost inevitable to speak of him after speaking of Mr. Abbey, for the definite reason (I hope that in giving it I may not appear to invade too grossly the domain of private life) that these gentlemen are united in domestic circumstance as well as associated in the nature of their work. In London, in the relatively lucid air of Campden Hill, they dwell together, and their beautiful studios are side by side. However, there is a reason for commemorating Mr. Parsons' work which has nothing to do with the accidental—the simple fact that that work forms the richest illustration of the English landscape that is offered us to-day. Harper has for a long time past been full of Mr. Alfred Parsons, who has made the dense, fine detail of his native land familiar in far countries, amid scenery of a very different type. This is what the modern illustration can do when the ripeness of the modern sense is brought to it and the wood-cutter plays with difficulties as the brilliant Americans do to-day, following his original at a breakneck pace. An illusion is produced which, in its very completeness, makes one cast an uneasy eye over the dwindling fields that are still left to conquer. Such art as Alfred Parsons'— such an accomplished translation of local aspects, translated in its turn by cunning hands and diffused by a wonderful system of periodicity through vast and remote communities, has, I confess, in a peculiar degree, the effect that so many things have in this age of multiplication—that of suppressing intervals and differences and making the globe seem alarmingly small. Vivid and repeated evocations of English rural things—the meadows and lanes, the sedgy streams, the old orchards and timbered houses, the stout, individual, insular trees, the flowers under the hedge and in it and over it, the sweet rich country seen from the slope, the bend of the unformidable river, the actual romance of the castle against the sky, the place on the hill-side where the gray church begins to peep (a peaceful little grassy path leads up to it over a stile)—all this brings about a terrible displacement of the very objects that make pilgrimage a passion, and hurries forward that ambiguous advantage which I don't envy our grandchildren, that of knowing all about everything in advance, having trotted round the globe annually in the magazines and lost the bloom of personal experience. It is a part of the general abolition of mystery with which we are all so complacently busy today. One would like to retire to another planet with a box of Mr. Parsons' drawings, and be homesick there for the pleasant places they commemorate.

There are many things to be said about his talent, some of which are not the easiest in the world to express. I shall not, however, make them more difficult by attempting to catalogue his contributions in these pages. A turning of the leaves of Harper brings one constantly face to face with him, and a systematic search speedily makes one intimate. The reader will remember the beautiful Illustrations to Mr. Blackmore's novel of *Springhaven*, which were interspersed with striking figure-pieces from the pencil of that very peculiar pictorial humorist Mr. Frederick Barnard, who, allowing for the fact that he always seems a little too much to be drawing for Dickens and that the footlights are the illumination of his scenic world, has so remarkable a sense of English types and attitudes, costumes and accessories, in what may be called the great-coat-and-gaiters period—the period when people were stiff with riding and wicked conspiracies went forward in sanded provincial inn-parlors. Mr. Alfred Parsons, who is still conveniently young, waked to his first vision of pleasant material in the comprehensive county of Somerset—a capital centre of impression for a painter of the bucolic. He has been to America; he has even reproduced with remarkable discrimination and truth some of the way-side objects of that country, not making them look in the least like their English equivalents, if equivalents they may be said to have. Was it there that Mr. Parsons learned so well how Americans would like England to appear? I ask this idle question simply because the England of his pencil, and not less of his brush (of his eminent brush there would be much to say), is exactly the England that the American imagination, restricted to itself, constructs from the poets, the novelists, from all the delightful testimony it inherits. It was scarcely to have been supposed possible that the native point of view would embrace and observe so many of the things that the more or less famished outsider is, in vulgar parlance, "after." In other words (though I appear to utter a foolish paradox), the danger might have been that Mr. Parsons knew his subject too well to feel it—to feel it, I mean, *à l'Américaine*. He is as tender of it as if he were vague about it, and as certain of it as if he were *blasé*.

But after having wished that his country should be just so, we proceed to discover that it is in fact not a bit different. Between these phases of our consciousness he is an unfailing messenger. The reader will remember how often he has accompanied with pictures the text of some amiable paper describing a pastoral region—Warwickshire or Surrey. Devonshire or the Thames. He will remember his exquisite designs for certain of Wordsworth's sonnets. A sonnet of Wordsworth is a difficult thing to illustrate, but Mr. Parsons' ripe taste has shown him the way. Then there are lovely morsels from his hand associated with the drawings of his friend Mr. Abbey—head-pieces, tailpieces, vignettes, charming combinations of flower and foliage, decorative clusters of all sorts of pleasant rural emblems. If he has an inexhaustible feeling for the country in general, his love of the myriad English flowers is perhaps the fondest part of it. He draws them with a rare perfection, and always—little definite, delicate, tremulous things as they are—with a certain nobleness. This latter quality, indeed. I am prone to find in all his work, and I should insist on it still more if I might refer to his important paintings. So composite are the parts of which any distinguished talent is made up that we have to feel our way as we enumerate them; and yet that very ambiguity is a challenge to analysis and to characterization. This "nobleness" on Mr. Parsons' part is the element of style—something large and manly, expressive of the total character of his facts. His landscape is the landscape of the male vision, and yet his touch is full of sentiment, of curiosity and endearment. These things, and others besides, make him the most interesting, the most living, of the new workers in his line. And what shall I say of the other things besides? How can I take precautions enough to say that among the new workers, deeply English as he is, there is comparatively something French in his manner? Many people will like him because they see in him—or they think they do—a certain happy mean. Will they not fancy they catch him taking the middle way between the unsociable French *étude* and the old-fashioned English "picture"? If one of these extremes is a desert, the other, no doubt, is an oasis still more vain. I have a recollection of productions of Mr. Alfred Parsons' which might have come from a Frenchman who was in love with English river-sides. I call to mind no studies—if he has made any—of French scenery; but if I did they would doubtless appear English enough. It is the fashion among sundry to maintain that the English landscape is of no use for *la peinture sérieuse*, that it is wanting in technical accent and is in general too storytelling, too self-conscious and dramatic also too lumpish and stodgy, of a green—*d'un vert bête*—which, when reproduced, looks like that of the chromo. Certain it is that there are many hands which are not to be trusted with it, and taste and integrity have been known to go down before it. But Alfred Parsons may be pointed to as one who has made the luxuriant and lovable things of his own country almost as "serious" as those familiar objects—the pasture and the poplar—which, even when infinitely repeated by the great school across the Channel, strike us as but meagre morsels of France.

V

In speaking of Mr. George H. Boughton, A.R.A., I encounter the same difficulty as with Mr. Millet: I find the window closed through which alone almost it is just to take a view of his talent. Mr. Boughton is a painter about whom there is little that is new to tell to-day, so conspicuous and incontestable is his achievement, the fruit of a career of which the beginning was not yesterday. He is a draughtsman and an illustrator only on occasion and by accident. These accidents have mostly occurred, however, in the pages of Harper, and the happiest of them will still be fresh in the memory of its readers. In the *Sketching Rambles in Holland* Mr. Abbey was a participant (as witness, among many things, the admirable drawing of the old Frisian woman bent over her Bible in church, with the heads of the burghers just visible above the rough archaic pew-tops—a drawing opposite to page 112 in the handsome volume into which these contributions were eventually gathered together); but most of the sketches were Mr. Boughton's, and the charming, amusing text is altogether his, save in the sense that it commemorates his companion's impressions as well as his own—the delightful, irresponsible, visual, sensual, pictorial, capricious impressions of a painter in a strange land, the person surely whom at particular moments one would give most to be. If there be anything happier than the impressions of a painter, it is the impressions of two, and the combination is set forth with uncommon spirit and humor in this frank record of the innocent lust of the eyes. Mr. Boughton scruples little, in general, to write as well as to draw, when the fancy takes him; to write in the manner of painters, with the bold, irreverent, unconventional, successful brush. If I were not afraid of the patronizing tone I would say that there is little doubt that if as a painter he had not had to try to write in character, he would certainly have made a characteristic writer. He has the most enviable "finds," not dreamed of in timid literature, yet making capital descriptive prose. Other specimens of them may be encountered in two or three Christmas tales, signed with the name whose usual place is the corner of a valuable canvas.

If Mr. Boughton is in this manner not a simple talent, further complications and reversions may be observed in him, as, for instance, that having reverted from America, where he spent his early years, back to England, the land of his origin, he has now in a sense oscillated again from the latter to the former country. He came to London one day years ago (from Paris, where he had been eating nutritively of the tree of artistic knowledge), in order to re-embark on the morrow for the United States; but that morrow never came—it has never come yet. Certainly now it never *can* come, for the country that Mr. Boughton left behind him in his youth is no longer there; the "old New York" is no longer a port to sail to, unless for phantom ships. In imagination, however, the author of "The Return of the *Mayflower*" has several times taken his way back; he has painted with conspicuous charm and success various episodes of the early Puritan story. He was able on occasion to remember vividly enough the low New England coast and the thin New England air. He has been perceptibly an inventor, calling into being certain types of face and dress, certain tones and associations of color (all in the line of what I should call subdued harmonies if I were not afraid of appearing to talk a jargon), which people are hungry for when they acquire "a Boughton," and which they can obtain on no other terms. This pictorial element in which he moves is made up of divers delicate things, and there would be a roughness in attempting to unravel the tapestry. There is old English, and old American, and old Dutch in it, and a friendly, unexpected new Dutch too—an ingredient of New Amsterdam—a strain of Knickerbocker and of Washington Irving. There is an admirable infusion of landscape in it, from which some people regret that Mr. Boughton should ever have allowed himself to be distracted by his importunate love of sad-faced, pretty women in close-fitting coifs and old silver-clasped cloaks. And indeed, though his figures are very "tender," his landscape is to my sense tenderer still. Moreover, Mr. Boughton bristles, not aggressively, but in the degree of a certain conciliatory pertinacity, with contradictious properties. He lives in one of the prettiest and most hospitable houses in London, but the note of his work is the melancholy of rural things, of lonely people and of quaint, far-off legend and refrain. There is a delightful ambiguity of period and even of clime in him, and he rejoices in that inability to depict the modern which is the most convincing sign of the contemporary.

He has a genius for landscape, yet he abounds in knowledge of every sort of ancient fashion of garment; the buckles and button-holes, the very shoe-ties, of the past are dear to him. It is almost always autumn or winter in his pictures. His horizons are cold, his trees are bare (he does the bare tree beautifully), and his draperies lined with fur; but when he exhibits himself directly, as in the fantastic "Rambles" before mentioned, contagious high spirits are the clearest of his showing. Here he appears as an irrepressible felicitous sketcher, and I know no pleasanter record of the joys of sketching, or even of those of simply looking. Théophile Gautier himself was not more inveterately addicted to this latter wanton exercise. There ought to be a pocket edition of Mr. Boughton's book, which would serve for travellers in other countries too, give them the point of view and put them in the mood. Such a blessing, and such a distinction too, is it to have an eye. Mr. Boughton's, in his good-humored Dutch wanderings, holds from morning till night a sociable, graceful revel. From the moment it opens till the moment it closes, its day is a round of adventures. His jolly pictorial narrative, reflecting every glint of October sunshine and patch of russet shade, tends to confirm us afresh in the faith that the painter's life is the best life, the life that misses fewest impressions.

VI

Mr. Du Maurier has a brilliant history, but it must be candidly recognized that it is written or drawn mainly in an English periodical. It is only during the last two or three years that the most ironical of the artists of *Punch* has exerted himself for the entertainment of the readers of Harper; but I seem to come too late with any commentary on the nature of his satire or the charm of his execution. When he began to appear in Harper he was already an old friend, and for myself I confess I have to go through rather a complicated mental operation to put into words what I think of him. What does a man think of the language he has learned to speak? He judges it only while he is learning. Mr. Du Maurier's work, in regard to the life it embodies, is not so much a thing we see as one of the conditions of seeing. He has interpreted for us for so many years the social life of England that the interpretation has become the text itself. We have accepted his types, his categories, his conclusions, his sympathies and his ironies, It is not given to all the world to thread the mazes of London society, and for the great body of the disinherited, the vast majority of the Anglo-Saxon public. Mr. Du Maurier's representation is the thing represented. Is the effect of it to nip in the bud any remote yearning for personal participation? I feel tempted to say yes, when I think of the follies, the flatnesses, the affectations and stupidities that his teeming pencil has made vivid. But that vision immediately merges itself in another—a panorama of tall, pleasant, beautiful people, placed in becoming attitudes, in charming gardens, in luxurious rooms, so that I can scarcely tell which is the more definite, the impression satiric or the impression plastic.

This I take to be a sign that Mr. Du Maurier knows how to be general and has a conception of completeness. The world amuses him, such queer things go on in it; but the part that amuses him most is certain lines of our personal structure. That amusement is the brightest; the other is often sad enough. A sharp critic might accuse Mr. Du Maurier of lingering too complacently on the lines in question; of having a certain ideal of "lissome" elongation to which the promiscuous truth is sometimes sacrificed. But in fact this artist's P truth never pretends to be promiscuous; it is avowedly select and specific. What he depicts is so preponderantly the "tapering" people that the remainder of the picture, in a notice as brief as the present, may be neglected. If his *dramatis personæ* are not all the tenants of drawing-rooms, they are represented at least in some relation to these. 'Arry and his friends at the fancy fair are in society for the time; the point of introducing them is to show how the contrast intensifies them. Of late years Mr. Du Maurier has perhaps been a little too docile to the muse of elegance; the idiosyncrasies of the "masher" and the high girl with elbows have beguiled him into occasional inattention to the doings of the short and shabby. But his career has been long and rich, and I allude, in such words, but to a moment of it.

The moral of it—I refer to the artistic one—seen altogether, is striking and edifying enough. What Mr. Du Maurier has attempted to do is to give, in a thousand interrelated drawings, a general satiric picture of the social life of his time and country. It is easy to see that through them "an increasing purpose runs;" they all hang together and refer to each other—complete, confirm, correct, illuminate each other. Sometimes they are not satiric: satire is not pure charm, and the artist has allowed himself to "go in" for pure charm. Sometimes he has allowed himself to go in for pure fantasy, so that satire (which should hold on to the mane of the real) slides off the other side of the runaway horse. But he remains, on the whole, pencil in hand, a wonderfully copious and veracious historian of his age and his civilization.

VII

I have left Mr. Reinhart to the last because of his importance, and now this very importance operates as a restriction and even as a sort of reproach to me. To go well round him at a deliberate pace would take a whole book. With Mr. Abbey, Mr. Reinhart is the artist who has contributed most abundantly to Harper; his work, indeed, in quantity, considerably exceeds Mr. Abbey's. He is the observer of the immediate, as Mr. Abbey is that of the considerably removed, and the conditions he asks us to accept are less expensive to the imagination than those of his colleague. He is, in short, the vigorous, racy *prosateur* of that human comedy of which Mr. Abbey is the poet. He illustrates the modern sketch of travel, the modern tale—the poor little "quiet," psychological, conversational modern tale, which I often think the artist invited to represent it to the eye must hate, unless he be a very intelligent master, little, on a superficial view, would there appear to be in it to represent. The superficial view is, after all, the natural one for the picture-maker. A talent of the first order, however, only wants to be set thinking, as a single word will often make it. Mr. Reinhart at any rate, triumphs; whether there be life or not in the little tale itself, there is unmistakable life in his version of it. Mr. Reinhart deals in that element purely with admirable frankness and vigor. He is not so much suggestive as positively and sharply representative. His facility, his agility, his universality are a truly stimulating sight. He asks not too many questions of his subject, but to those he does ask he insists upon a thoroughly intelligible answer. By his universality I mean perhaps as much as anything else his admirable drawing; not precious, as the æsthetic say, nor pottering, as the vulgar, but free, strong and secure, which enables him to do with the human figure at a moment's notice anything that any occasion may demand. It gives him an immense range, and I know not how to express (it is not easy) my sense of a certain capable indifference that is in him otherwise than by saying that he would quite as soon do one thing as another.

For it is true that the admirer of his work rather misses in him that intimation of a secret preference which many strong draughtsmen show, and which is not absent, for instance (I don't mean the secret, but the intimation), from the beautiful doings of Mr. Abbey. It is extremely present in Mr. Du Maurier's work, just as it was visible, less elusively, in that of John Leech, his predecessor in *Punch*. Mr. Abbey has a haunting type; Du Maurier has a haunting type. There was little perhaps of the haunted about Leech, but we know very well how he wanted his pretty girls, his British swell, and his "hunting men" to look. He betrayed a predilection; he had his little ideal. That an artist may be a great force and not have a little ideal, the scarcely too much to be praised Charles Keene is there (I mean he is in *Punch*) to show us. He has not a haunting type—not he—and I think that no one has yet discovered how he would have liked his pretty girls to look. He has kept the soft conception too much to himself—he has not trifled with the common truth by letting it appear. This common truth, in its innumerable combinations, is what Mr. Rein-hart also shows us (with of course infinitely less of a *parti pris* of laughing at it), though, as I must hasten to add, the female face and form in his hands always happen to take on a much lovelier cast than in Mr. Keene's. These things with him, however, are not a private predilection, an artist's dream. Mr. Reinhart is solidly an artist, but I doubt whether as yet he dreams, and the absence of private predilections makes him seem a little hard. He is sometimes rough with our average humanity, and especially rough with the feminine portion of it. He usually represents American life, in which that portion is often spoken of as showing to peculiar advantage. But Mr. Reinhart sees it generally, as very *bourgeois*. His good ladies are apt to be rather thick and short, rather huddled and plain. I shouldn't mind it so much if they didn't look so much alive. They are incontestably possible. The long, brilliant series of drawings he made to accompany Mr. Charles Dudley Warner's papers on the American watering-places form a rich *bourgeois* epic, which imaginations haunted by a type must accept with philosophy, for the sketches in question will have carried the tale, and all sorts of irresistible illusion with it, to the four corners of the earth. Full of observation and reality, of happy impressionism, taking all things as they come, with many a charming picture of youthful juxtaposition, they give us a sense, to which nothing need be added, of the energy of Mr. Reinhart's pencil. They are a final collection of pictorial notes on the manners and customs, the aspects and habitats, in July and August, of the great American democracy; of which, certainly, taking one thing with another, they give a very comfortable, cheerful account. But they confirm that analytic view of which I have ventured to give a hint—the view of Mr. Reinhart as an artist of immense capacity who yet somehow doesn't care. I must add that this aspect of him is modified, in the one case very gracefully, in the other by the operation of a sort of constructive humor, remarkably strong, in his illustrations of Spanish life and his sketches of the Berlin political world.

His fashion of remaining outside, as it were, makes him (to the analyst) only the more interesting, for the analyst, if he have any critical life in him, will be prone to wonder *why* he doesn't care, and whether matters may not be turned about in such a way as that he should, with the consequence that his large capacity would become more fruitful still. Mr. Reinhart is open to the large appeal of Paris, where he lives—as is evident from much of his work—where he paints, and where, in crowded exhibitions, reputation and honors have descended upon him. And yet Paris, for all she may have taught him, has not given him the mystic sentiment—about which I am perhaps writing nonsense. Is it nonsense to say that, being very much an incarnation of the modern international spirit (he might be a Frenchman in New York were he not an American in Paris), the moral of his work is possibly the inevitable want of finality, of intrinsic character, in that sweet freedom? Does the cosmopolite necessarily pay for his freedom by a want of function—the impersonality of not being representative? Must one be a little narrow to have a sentiment, and very local to have a quality, or at least a style; and would the missing type, if I may mention it yet again, haunt our artist—who is somehow, in his rare instrumental facility, outside of quality and style—a good deal more if he were not, amid the mixture of associations and the confusion of races, liable to fall into vagueness as to what types are? He can do anything he likes; by which I mean he can do wonderfully even the things he doesn't like. But he strikes me as a force not yet fully used.

EDWIN A. ABBE

Nothing is more interesting in the history of an artistic talent than the moment at which its "elective affinity" declares itself, and the interest is great in proportion as the declaration is unmistakable. I mean by the elective affinity of a talent its climate and period of preference, the spot on the globe or in the annals of mankind to which it most fondly attaches itself, to which it reverts incorrigibly, round which it revolves with a curiosity that is insatiable, from which in short it draws its strongest inspiration. A man may personally inhabit a certain place at a certain time, but in imagination he may be a perpetual absentee, and to a degree worse than the worst Irish landlord, separating himself from his legal inheritance not only by mountains and seas, but by centuries as well. When he is a man of genius these perverse predilections become fruitful and constitute a new and independent life, and they are indeed to a certain extent the sign and concomitant of genius. I do not mean by this that high ability would always rather have been born in another country and another age, but certainly it likes to choose, it seldom fails to react against imposed conditions. If it accepts them it does so because it likes them for themselves; and if they fail to commend themselves it rarely scruples to fly away in search of others. We have witnessed this flight in many a case; I admit that if we have sometimes applauded it we have felt at other moments that the discontented, undomiciled spirit had better have stayed at home.

Mr. Abbey has gone afield, and there could be no better instance of a successful fugitive and a genuine affinity, no more interesting example of selection—selection of field and subject—operating by that insight which has the precocity and certainty of an instinct. The domicile of Mr. Abbey's genius is the England of the eighteenth century; I should add that the palace of art which he has erected there commands—from the rear, as it were—various charming glimpses of the preceding age. The finest work he has yet done is in his admirable illustrations, in Harper's Magazine, to "She Stoops to Conquer," but the promise that he would one day do it was given some years ago in his delightful volume of designs to accompany Herrick's poems; to which we may add, as supplementary evidence, his drawings for Mr. William Black's novel of *Judith Shakespeare.*

Mr. Abbey was born in Philadelphia in 1852, and manifesting his brilliant but un-encouraged aptitudes at a very early age, came in 1872 to New York to draw for Harper's WEEKLY. Other views than this, if I have been correctly Informed, had been entertained for his future—a fact that provokes a smile now that his manifest destiny has been, or is in course of being, so very neatly accomplished. The spirit of modern aesthetics did not, at any rate, as I understand the matter, smile upon his cradle, and the circumstance only increases the interest of his having had from the earliest moment the clearest artistic vision.

It has sometimes happened that the distinguished draughtsman or painter has been born in the studio and fed, as it were, from the palette, but in the great majority of cases he has been nursed by the profane, and certainly, on the doctrine of mathematical chances, a Philadelphia genius would scarcely be an exception. Mr. Abbey was fortunate, however, in not being obliged to lose time; he learned how to swim by jumping into deep water. Even if he had not known by instinct how to draw, he would have had to perform the feat from the moment that he found himself attached to the "art department" of a remarkably punctual periodical. In such a periodical the events of the day are promptly reproduced; and with the morrow so near the day is necessarily a short one—too short for gradual education. Such a school is not, no doubt, the ideal one, but in fact it may have a very happy influence. If a youth is to give an account of a scene with his pencil at a certain hour—to give it, as it were, or perish—he will have become conscious, in the first place, of a remarkable incentive to observe it. so that the roughness of the foster-mother who imparts the precious faculty of quick, complete observation is really a blessing in disguise. To say that it was simply under this kind of pressure that Mr. Abbey acquired the extraordinary refinement which distinguishes his work in black and white is doubtless to say too much; but his admirers may be excused, in view of the beautiful result, for almost wishing, on grounds of patriotism, to make the training, or the absence of training, responsible for as much as possible. For as no artistic genius that our country has produced is more delightful than Mr. Abbey's, so, surely, nothing could be more characteristically American than that it should have formed itself in the conditions that happened to be nearest at hand, with the crowds, streets and squares, the railway stations and telegraph poles, the wondrous sign-boards and triumphant bunting, of New York for the source of its inspiration, and with a big hurrying printing-house for its studio. If to begin the practice of art in these conditions was to incur the danger of being crude, Mr. Abbey braved it with remarkable success. At all events, if he went neither I through the mill of Paris nor through that of Munich, the writer of these lines more than consoles himself for the accident. His talent is unsurpassably fine, and yet we reflect with complacency that he picked it up altogether at home. If he is highly distinguished he is irremediably native, and (premising always that I speak mainly of his work in black and white) it is difficult to see, as we look, for instance, at the admirable series of his drawings for "She Stoops to Conquer," what more Paris or Munich could have done for him. There is a certain refreshment in meeting an American artist of the first order who is not a pupil of Gérôme or of Cabanel.

Of course, I hasten to add, we must make our account with the fact that, as I began with remarking, the great development of Mr. Abbey's powers has taken place amid the brown old accessories of a country where that eighteenth century which he presently marked for his own are more profusely represented than they have the good-fortune to be in America, and consequently limit our contention to the point that his talent itself was already formed when this happy initiation was opened to it. He went to England for the first time in 1878. but it was not all at once that he fell into the trick, so irresistible for an artist doing his special work, of living there, I must forbid myself every impertinent conjecture, but it may be respectfully assumed that Mr. Abbey rather drifted into exile than committed himself to it with malice prepense. The habit, at any rate, to-day appears to be confirmed, and, to express it roughly, he is surrounded by the utensils and conveniences that he requires. During these years, until the recent period when he began to exhibit at the water-color exhibitions, his work has been done principally for Harper's Magazine, and the record of it is to be found in the recent back volumes. I shall not take space to tell it over piece by piece, for the reader who turns to the Magazine will have no difficulty in recognizing it. It has a distinction altogether its own; there is always poetry, humor, charm, in the idea, and always infinite grace and security in the execution.

As I have intimated, Mr. Abbey never deals with the things and figures of to-day; his imagination must perform a wide backward journey before it can take the air. But beyond this modern radius it breathes with singular freedom and naturalness. At a distance of fifty years it begins to be at home; it expands and takes possession; it recognizes its own. With all his ability, with all his tact, it would be impossible to him, we conceive, to illustrate a novel of contemporary manners; he would inevitably throw it back to the age of hair-powder and post-chaises. The coats and trousers, the feminine gear, the chairs and tables of the current year, the general aspect of things immediate and familiar, say nothing to his mind, and there are other interpreters to whom he is quite content to leave them. He shows no great interest even in the modern face, if there be a modern face apart from a modern setting; I am not sure what he thinks of its complications and refinements of expression, but he has certainly little relish for its *banal*, vulgar mustache, its prosaic, mercantile whisker, surmounting the last new thing in shirt-collars. Dear to him is the physiognomy of clean-shaven periods, when cheek and lip and chin, abounding in line and surface, had the air of soliciting the pencil. Impeccable as he is in drawing, he likes a whole face, with reason, and likes a whole figure; the latter not to the exclusion of clothes, in which he delights, but as the clothes of our great-grandfathers helped it to be seen. No one has ever understood breeches and stockings better than he, or the human leg, that delight of the draughtsman, as the costume of the last century permitted it to be known. The petticoat and bodice of the same period have as little mystery for him, and his women and girls have altogether the poetry of a by-gone manner and fashion. They are not modern heroines, with modern nerves and accomplishments, but figures of remembered song and story, calling up visions of spinet and harpsichord that have lost their music today, high-walled gardens that have ceased to bloom, flowered stuffs that are faded, locks of hair that are lost, love-letters that are pale. By which I don't mean that they are vague and spectral, for Mr. Abbey has in the highest degree the art of imparting life, and he gives it in particular to his well-made, blooming maidens. They live in a world in which there is no question of their passing Harvard or other examinations, but they stand very firmly on their quaintly-shod feet. They are exhaustively "felt," and eminently qualified to attract the opposite sex, which is not the case with ghosts, who, moreover, do not wear the most palpable petticoats of quilted satin, nor sport the most delicate fans, nor take generally the most ingratiating attitudes.

The best work that Mr. Abbey has done is to be found in the succession of illustrations to "She Stoops to Conquer;" here we see his happiest characteristics and—till he does something still more brilliant—may take his full measure. No work in black and white in our time has been more truly artistic, and certainly no success more unqualified. The artist has given us an evocation of a social state to its smallest details, and done it with an unsurpassable lightness of touch. The problem was in itself delightful—the accidents and incidents (granted a situation *de comédie*) of an old, rambling, wainscoted, out-of-the-way English country-house, in the age of Goldsmith. Here Mr. Abbey is in his element—given up equally to unerring observation and still more infallible divination. The whole place, and the figures that come and go in it, live again, with their individual look, their peculiarities, their special signs and oddities. The spirit of the dramatist has passed completely into the artist's sense, but the spirit of the historian has done so almost as much. Tony Lumpkin is, as we say nowadays, a document, and Miss Hardcastle embodies the results of research. Delightful are the humor and quaintness and grace of all this, delightful the variety and the richness of personal characterization, and delightful, above all, the drawing. It is impossible to represent with such vividness unless, to begin with, one sees; and it is impossible to see unless one wants to very much, or unless, in other words, one has a great love. Mr. Abbey has evidently the tenderest affection for just the old houses and the old things, the old faces and voices, the whole irrevocable human scene which the genial hand of Goldsmith has passed over to him, and there is no inquiry about them that he is not in a position to answer. He is intimate with the buttons of coats and the buckles of shoes: he knows not only exactly what his people wore, but exactly how they wore it, and how they felt when they had it on. He has sat on the old chairs and sofas, and rubbed against the old wainscots, and leaned over the old balusters. He knows every mended place in Tony Lumpkin's stockings, and exactly how that ingenuous youth leaned back on the spinet, with his thick, familiar thumb out, when he presented his inimitable countenance, with a grin, to Mr. Hastings, after he had set his fond mother a-whimpering. (There is nothing in the whole series, by-the-way, better indicated than the exquisitely simple, half-bumpkin, half-vulgar expression of Tony's countenance and smile in this scene, unless it be the charming arch yet modest face of Miss Hardcastle, lighted by the candle she carries, as, still holding the door by which she comes in, she is challenged by young Mar-low to relieve his bewilderment as to where he really is and what *she* really is.) In short, if we have all seen "She Stoops to Conquer" acted, Mr. Abbey has had the better fortune of seeing it off the stage; and it is noticeable how happily he has steered clear of the danger of making his people theatrical types—mere masqueraders and wearers of properties. This is especially the case with his women, who have not a hint of the conventional paint and patches, simpering with their hands in the pockets of aprons, but are taken from the same originals from which Goldsmith took them.

If it be asked on the occasion of this limited sketch of Mr. Abbey's powers where, after all, he did learn to draw so perfectly, I know no answer but to say that he learned it in the school in which he learned also to paint (as he has been doing in these latest years, rather tentatively at first, but with greater and greater success)—the school of his own personal observation. His drawing is the drawing of direct, immediate, solicitous study of the particular case, without tricks or affectations or any sort of cheap subterfuge, and nothing can exceed the charm of its delicacy, accuracy and elegance, its variety and freedom, its clear, frank solution of difficulties. If for the artist it be the foundation of every joy to know exactly what he wants (as I hold it is indeed), Mr. Abbey is, to all appearance, to be constantly congratulated. And I apprehend that he would not deny that it is a good-fortune for him to have been able to arrange his life so that his eye encounters in abundance the particular cases of which I speak. Two or three years ago, at the Institute of Painters in Water-colors, in London, he exhibited an exquisite picture of a peaceful old couple sitting in the corner of a low, quiet, ancient room, in the waning afternoon, and listening to their daughter as she stands up in the middle and plays the harp to them. They are Darby and Joan, with all the poetry preserved; they sit hand in hand, with bent, approving heads, and the deep recess of the window looking into the garden (where we may be sure there are yew-trees clipped into the shape of birds and beasts), the panelled room, the quaintness of the fireside, the old-time provincial expression of the scene, all belong to the class of effects which Mr. Abbey understands supremely well. So does the great russet wall and high-pitched mottled roof of the rural almshouse which figures in the admirable water-color picture that he exhibited last spring. A group of remarkably pretty countrywomen have been arrested in front of it by the passage of a young soldier—a raw recruit in scarlet tunic and white ducks, somewhat prematurely conscious of military glory. He gives them the benefit of the goose-step as he goes; he throws back his head and distends his fingers, presenting to the ladies a back expressive of more consciousness of his fine figure than of the lovely mirth that the artist has depicted in their faces. Lovely is their mirth indeed, and lovely are they altogether. Mr. Abbey has produced nothing more charming than this bright knot of handsome, tittering daughters of burghers, in their primeval pelisses and sprigged frocks. I have, however, left myself no space to go into the question of his prospective honors as a painter, to which everything now appears to point, and I have mentioned the two pictures last exhibited mainly because they illustrate the happy opportunities with which he has been able to surround himself. The sweet old corners he appreciates, the russet walls of moss-grown charities, the lowbrowed nooks of manor, cottage and parsonage, the fresh complexions that flourish in green, pastoral countries where it rains not a little—every item in this line that seems conscious of its pictorial use appeals to Mr. Abbey not in vain. He might have been a grandson of Washington Irving, which is a proof of what I have already said, that none of the young American workers in the same field have so little as he of that imperfectly assimilated foreignness of suggestion which is sometimes regarded as the strength, but which is also in some degree the weakness, of the pictorial effort of the United States. His execution is as sure of itself as if it rested upon infinite Parisian initiation, but his feeling can best be described by saying that it is that of our own dear mother-tongue. If the writer speaks when he writes, and the draughtsman speaks when he draws. Mr. Abbey, in expressing himself with his pencil, certainly speaks pure English, He reminds us to a certain extent of Meissonier, especially the Meissonier of the illustrations to that charming little volume of the *Conies Rémois*, and the comparison is highly to his advantage in the matter of freedom, variety, ability to represent movement (Meissonier's figures are stock-still), and facial expression—above all, in the handling of the female personage, so rarely attempted by the French artist. But he differs from the latter signally in the fact that though he shares his sympathy as to period and costume, his people are of another race and tradition, and move in a world locally altogether different. Mr. Abbey is still young, he is full of ideas and intentions, and the work he has done may, in view of his time of life, of his opportunities and the singular completeness of his talent, be regarded really as a kind of foretaste and prelude. It can hardly fail that he will do better things still, when everything is so favorable. Life itself is his subject, and that is always at his door. The only obstacle, therefore, that can be imagined in Mr. Abbey's future career is a possible embarrassment as to what to choose. He has hitherto chosen so well, however, that this obstacle will probably not be insuperable.

CHARLES S. REINHART

We Americans are accused of making too much ado about our celebrities, of being demonstratively conscious of each step that we take in the path of progress; and the accusation has its ground doubtless in this sense, that it is possible among us to-day to become a celebrity on unprecedentedly easy terms. This, however, at the present hour is the case all the world over, and it is difficult to see where the standard of just renown remains so high that the first stone may be cast. It is more and more striking that the machinery of publicity is so enormous, so constantly growing and so obviously destined to make the globe small, in relation of the objects, famous or obscure, which cover it, that it procures for the smallest facts and the most casual figures a reverberation to be expected only in the case of a world-conqueror. The newspaper and the telegram constitute a huge sounding-board, which has, every day and every hour, to be made to vibrate, to be fed with items, and the diffusion of the items takes place on a scale out of any sort of proportion to their intrinsic importance. The crackle of common things is transmuted into thunder—a thunder perhaps more resounding in America than elsewhere for the reason that the sheet of tin shaken by the Jupiter of the Press has been cut larger. But the difference is only of degree, not of kind; and if the system we in particular have brought to perfection would seem to be properly applied only to Alexanders and Napoleons, it is not striking that these adequate subjects present themselves even in other countries. The end of it all surely no man can see, unless it be that collective humanity is destined to perish from a rupture of its tympanum. That is a theme for a later hour, and meanwhile perhaps it is well not to be too frightened. Some of the items I just spoke of are, after all, larger than others; and if, as a general thing, it is a mistake to pull up our reputations to see how they are growing, there are some so well grown that they will bear it, and others of a hardy stock even while they are tender. We may feel, for instance, comparatively little hesitation in extending an importunate hand towards the fine young sapling of which Mr. Reinhart is one of the branches. It is a plant of promise, which has already flowered profusely and the fragrance of which it would be affectation not to to notice. Let us notice it, then, with candor, for it has all the air of being destined to make the future sweeter. The plant in question is of course simply the art of illustration in black and white, to which American periodical literature has, lately given such an impetus and which has returned the good office by conferring a great distinction on our magazines. In its new phase the undertaking has succeeded; and it is not always that fortune descends upon so deserving a head. Two or three fine talents in particular have helped it to succeed, and Mr. Reinhart is not the least conspicuous of these. It would be idle for a writer in Harper to pretend to any diffidence of appreciation of his work: for the pages are studded, from many years back, with the record of his ability. Mr. Rein-hart took his first steps and made his first hits in Harper, which owes him properly a portrait in return for so much portraiture. I may exaggerate the charm and the importance of the modern illustrative form, may see in it a capacity of which it is not yet itself wholly conscious, but if I do so Mr. Reinhart is partly responsible for the aberration. Abundant, intelligent, interpretative work in black and white is, to the sense of the writer of these lines, one of the pleasantest things of the time, having only to rise to the occasion to enjoy a great future. This idea, I confess, is such as to lead one to write not only sympathetically but pleadingly about the artists to whom one looks for confirmation of it. If at the same time as we commemorate what they have done we succeed in enlarging a little the conception of what they may yet do, we shall be repaid even for having exposed ourselves as fanatics— fanatics of the general manner, I mean, not of particular representatives of it.

May not this fanaticism, in a particular case, rest upon a sense of the resemblance between the general chance, as it may be called, of the draughtsman in black and white, with contemporary life for his theme, and the opportunity upon which the literary artist brings another form to bear? The forms are different, though with analogies; but the field is the same—the immense field of contemporary life observed for an artistic purpose. There is nothing so interesting as that, because it is ourselves; and no artistic problem is so charming as to arrive, either in a literary or a plastic form, at a close and direct notation of what we observe. If one has attempted some such exploit in a literary form, one cannot help having a sense of union and comradeship with those who have approached the question with the other instrument. This will be especially the case if we happen to have appreciated that instrument even to envy. We may as well say it outright, we envy it quite unspeakably in the hands of Mr. Reinhart and in those of Mr. Abbey. There is almost no limit to the service to which we can imagine it to be applied, and we find ourselves wishing that these gentlemen may be made adequately conscious of all the advantages it represents. We wonder whether they really *are* so; we are disposed even to assume that they are not, in order to join the moral, to insist on the lesson. The master whom we have mentally in view Mr. Reinhart is a near approach to him may be, if he will only completely know it, so prompt, so copious, so universal—so "all there," as we say nowadays, and indeed so all everywhere. There is only too much to see, too much to do, and his process is the one that comes nearest to minimizing the quantity. He can touch so many things, he can go from one scene to another, he can sound a whole concert of notes while the painter is setting up his easel. The painter is majestic, dignified, academic, important, superior, anything you will; but he is, in the very nature of the case, only occasional. He is "serious," but he is comparatively clumsy: he is a terrible time getting under way, and he has to sacrifice so many subjects while he is doing one. The illustrator makes one immense sacrifice, of course—that of color; but with it he purchases a freedom which enables him to attack ever so many ideas. It is by variety and numerosity that he commends himself to his age, and it is for these qualities that his age commends him to the next. The twentieth century, the latter half of it, will, no doubt, have its troubles, but it will have a great compensatory luxury, that of seeing the life of a hundred years before much more vividly than we—even happy we—see the life of a hundred years ago. But for this our illustrators must do their best, appreciate the endless capacity of their form. It is to the big picture what the short story is to the novel.

It is doubtless too much, I hasten to add, to ask Mr. Reinhart, for instance, to work to please the twentieth century. The end will not matter if he pursues his present very prosperous course of activity, for it is assuredly the fruitful vein, the one I express the hope to see predominant, the portrayal of the manners, types and aspects that surround us. Mr. Reinhart has reached that happy period of life when a worker is in full possession of his means, when he has done for his chosen instrument everything he can do in the way of forming it and rendering it complete and flexible, and has the fore only to apply it with freedom, confidence and success. These, to our sense, are the golden hours of an artist's life; happier even than the younger time when the future seemed infinite in the light of the first rays of glory, the first palpable hits. The very sense that the future is *not* unlimited and that opportunity is at its high-water-mark gives an intensity to the enjoyment of maturity. Then the acquired habit of "knowing how" must simplify the problem of execution and leave the artist free to think only of his purpose, as befits a real creator. Mr. Reinhart is at the enviable stage of knowing in perfection how; he has arrived at absolute facility and felicity. The machine goes of itself; it is no longer necessary to keep lifting the cover and pouring in the oil of fond encouragement: all the attention may go to the idea and the subject. It may, however, remain very interesting to others to know how the faculty was trained, the pipe was tuned. The early phases of such a process have a relative importance even when, at the lime (so gradual are many beginnings and so obscure man a morrow) they may have appeared neither delightful nor profitable. They are almost always to be summed up in the single precious word practice. This word represents, at any rate, Mr. Reinhart's youthful history, and the profusion in which, though no doubt occasionally disguised, the boon was supplied to him in the offices of Harper's Magazine. There is nothing so innate that it has not also to be learned, for the best part of any aptitude is the capacity to increase it.

Mr. Reinhart's experience began to accumulate very early, for at Pittsburgh, where he was born, he was free to draw to his heart's content. There was no romantic attempt, as I gather, to nip him in the bud. On the contrary, he was despatched with almost prosaic punctuality to Europe, and was even encouraged to make himself at home in Munich. Munich, in his case, was a *pis-aller* for Paris, where it would have been his preference to study when he definitely surrendered, as it were, to his symptoms. He went to Paris, but Paris seemed blocked and complicated, and Munich presented advantages which, if not greater, were at least easier to approach. Mr. Reinhart passe through the mill of the Bavarian school, and when it had turned him out with its characteristic polish he came back to America

44

with a very substantial stock to dispose of. It would take a chapter by itself if we were writing a biography, this now very usual episode of the return of the young American from the foreign conditions in which he has learned his professional language, and his position in face of the community that he addresses in a strange idiom. There has to be a prompt adjustment between ear and voice, if the interlocutor is not to seem to himself to be intoning in the void. There is always an inner history in all this, as well as an outer one— such, however, as it would take much space to relate. Mr. Reinhart's more or less alienated accent fell, by good-fortune, on a comprehending listener. He had made a satirical drawing, in the nature of the "cartoon" of a comic journal, on a subject of the hour, and addressed it to the editor of *Harper's Weekly*. The drawing was not published—the satire was perhaps not exactly on the right note—but the draughtsman was introduced. Thus began, by return of post, as it were, and with preliminaries so few that they could not well have been less, a connection of many years. If I were writing a biography another chapter would come in here—a curious, almost a pathetic one; for the course of things is so rapid in this country that the years of Mr. Reinhart's apprenticeship to pictorial journalism, positively recent as they are, already are almost prehistoric. To-morrow, at least, the complexion of that time, its processes, ideas and standards, together with some of the unsophisticated who carried them out, will belong to old New York. A certain mollifying dimness rests upon them now, and their superseded brilliancy gleams through it but faintly. It is a lively span for Mr. Reinhart to have been at once one of the unsophisticated and one of the actually modern.

That portion of his very copious work to which, more particularly. I apply the latter term, has been done for Harper's Magazine. During these latter years it has come, like so much of American work to-day, from beyond the seas. Whether or not that foreign language of which I just spoke never became, in New York, for this especial possessor of it, a completely convenient medium of conversation, is more than I can say; at any rate Mr. Reinhart eventually reverted to Europe and settled in Paris. Paris had seemed rather inhospitable to him in his youth, but he has now fitted his key to the lock. It would be satisfactory to be able to express scientifically the reasons why, as a general thing, the American artist, as well as his congener of many another land, carries on his function with less sense of resistance in that city than elsewhere. He likes Paris best, but that is not scientific. The difference is that though theoretically the production of pictures is recognized in America and in England, in Paris it is recognized both theoretically and practically. And I do not mean by this simply that pictures are bought—for they are not, predominantly, as it happens—but that they are more presupposed. The plastic is implied in the French conception of things, and the studio is as natural a consequence of it as the post-office is of letter-writing. Vivid representation is the genius of the French language and the need of the French mind. The people have invented more aids to it than any other, and as these aids make up a large part of the artist's life, he feels his best home to be in the place where he finds them most. He may begin to quarrel with that home on the day a complication is introduced by the question of *what* he shall represent—a totally different consideration from that of the method; but for Mr. Reinhart this question has not yet offered insoluble difficulties. He represents everything—he has accepted so general an order. So long as his countrymen flock to Paris and pass in a homogeneous procession before his eyes, there is not the smallest difficulty in representing *them*. When the case requires that they shall be taken in connection with their native circumstances and seen in their ambient air, he is prepared to come home and give several months to the task, as on the occasion of Mr. Dudley Warner's history of a tour among the watering-places, to which he furnished so rich and so curious a pictorial accompaniment. Sketch-book in hand, he betakes himself, according to need, to Germany, to England, to Italy, to Spain. The readers of Harper will have forgotten his admirable pictorial notes on the political world at Berlin, so rich and close in characterization. To the *Spanish Vistas* of Mr. G. P. Lathrop he contributed innumerable designs, delightful notes of an artist's quest of the sketchable, many of which are singularly full pictures. The "Soldiers Playing Dominoes" at a café is a powerful page of life. Mr. Reinhart has, of course, interpreted many a fictive scene—he has been repeatedly called upon to make the novel and the story visible. This he energetically and patiently does; though of course we are unable to say whether the men and women he makes us see are the very people whom the authors have seen. That is a thing that, in any case, one will never know; besides, the authors who don't see vaguely are apt to see perversely. The story-teller has, at any rate, the comfort with Mr. Reinhart that his drawings are constructive and have the air of the actual. He likes to represent character—he rejoices in the specifying touch.

The evidence of this is to be found also in his pictures, for I ought already to have mentioned that, for these many years (they are beginning to be many), he has indulged in the luxury of color. It is not probable that he regards himself in the first place as an illustrator, in the sense to which the term is usually restricted. He is a very vigorous and various painter, and at the Salon a constant and conspicuous exhibitor. He is fond of experiments, difficulties and dangers, and I divine that it would be his preference to be known best by his painting, in which he handles landscape with equal veracity. It is a pity that the critic is unable to contend with him on such a point without appearing to underestimate that work. Mr. Reinhart has so much to show for his preference that I am conscious of its taking some assurance to say that I am not sure he is right. This would be the case even if he had nothing else to show than the admirable picture entitled "Washed Ashore" ("Un Epave") which made such an impression in the Salon of 1887. It represents the dead body of an unknown man whom the tide has cast up, lying on his back, feet forward, disfigured, dishonored by the sea. A small group of villagers are collected near it, divided by the desire to look and the fear to see. A gendarme, official and responsible, his uniform contrasting with the mortal disrepair of the victim, takes down in his note-book the *procès-verbal* of the incident, and an old sailor, pointing away with a stiffened arm, gives him the benefit of what *he* knows about the matter. Plain, pitying, fish-wives, hushed, with their shawls in their mouths, hang back, as if from a combination too solemn—the mixture of death and the law. Three or four men seem to be glad it isn't they. The thing is a masterpiece of direct representation, and has wonderfully the air of something seen, found without being looked for. Excellently composed but not artificial, deeply touching but not sentimental, large, close and sober, this important work gives the full measure of Mr. Reinhart's great talent and constitutes a kind of pledge. It may be perverse on my part to see in it the big banknote, as it were, which may be changed into a multitude of gold and silver pieces. I cannot, however, help doing so. "Washed Ashore" is painted as only a painter paints, but I irreverently translate it into its equivalent in "illustrations"—half a hundred little examples, in black and white, of the same sort of observation. For this observation, immediate, familiar, sympathetic, human, and not involving a quest of style for which color is really indispensable, is a mistress at whose service there is no derogation in placing one's self. To do little things instead of big *may* be a derogation; a great deal will depend upon the way the little things are done. Besides, no work of art is absolutely little. I grow bold and even impertinent as I think of the way Mr. Rein-hart might scatter the smaller coin. At any rate, whatever proportion his work in this line may bear to the rest, it is to be hoped that nothing will prevent him from turning out more and more to play the rare faculty that produces it. His studies of American *moeurs* in association with Mr. Warner went so far on the right road that we would fain see him make all the rest of the journey. They made us ask straightway for more, and were full of intimations of what was behind. They showed what there is to see—what there is to guess. Let him carry the same inquiry further, let him carry it all the way. It would be serious work and would abound in reality; it would help us, as it were, to know what we are talking about. In saying this I feel how much I confirm the great claims I just made for the revival of illustration.

ALFRED PARSONS

It would perhaps be extravagant to pretend, in this embarrassed age, that Merry England is still intact; but it would be strange if the words "happy England" should not rise to the lips of the observer of Mr. Alfred Parsons' numerous and delightful studies of the gardens, great and small, of his country. They surely have a representative value in more than the literal sense, and might easily minister to the quietest complacency of patriotism. People whose criticism is imaginative will see in them a kind of compendium of what, in home things, is at once most typical and most enviable; and, going further, they will almost wish that such a collection might be carried by slow stages round the globe, to kindle pangs in the absent and passions in the alien. As it happens to be a globe the English race has largely peopled, we can measure the amount of homesickness that would be engendered on the way. In fact, one doubts whether the sufferer would even need to be of English strain to attach the vision of home to the essentially lovable places that Mr. Parsons depicts. They seem to generalize and typify the idea, so that every one may feel, in every case, that he has a sentimental property in the scene. The very sweetness of its reality only helps to give it that story-book quality which persuades us we have known it in youth.

And yet such scenes may well have been constructed for the despair of the Colonial; for they remind us, at every glance, of that perfection to which there is no short cut—not even "unexampled prosperity "—and to which time is the only guide. Mr. Parsons' pictures speak of many complicated things, but (in what they tell us of his subjects) they speak most of duration. Such happy nooks have grown slowly, such fortunate corners have had a history; and their fortune has been precisely that they have had time to have it comfortably, have not been obliged to try for character without it.

Character is their strong point and the most expensive of all ingredients. Mr. Parsons' portraiture seizes every shade of it, seizes it with unfailing sympathy. He is doubtless clever enough to paint rawness when he must, but he has an irrepressible sense of ripeness. Half the ripeness of England—half the religion, one might almost say—is in its gardens; they are truly pious foundations. It is doubtless because there are so many of them that the country seems so finished, and the sort of care they demand is an intenser deliberation, which passes into the national temper. One must have lived in other lands to observe fully how large a proportion of this one is walled in for growing flowers. The English love of flowers is inveterate; it is the most, unanimous protest against the grayness of some of the conditions, and it should receive justice from those who accuse the race of taking its pleasure too sadly. A good garden is an organized revel, and there is no country in which there are so many.

Mr. Parsons had therefore only to choose, at his leisure, and one might heartily have envied him the process, scarcely knowing which to prefer of all the pleasant pilgrimages that would make up such a quest. He had. fortunately, the knowledge which could easily lead to more, and a career of discovery behind him. He knew the right times for the right things, and the right things for the right places. He had innumerable memories and associations; he had painted up and down the land and looked over many walls. He had followed the bounty of the year from month to month and from one profusion to another. To follow it with him, in this admirable series, is to see that he is master of the subject. There will be no lack of confidence on the part of those who have already perceived, in much of Mr. Parsons' work, a supreme illustration of all that is widely nature-loving in the English interest in the flower. No sweeter submission to mastery can be imagined than the way the daffodils, under his brush (to begin at the beginning), break out into early April in the lovely drawings of Stourhead. One of the most charming of these—a corner of an old tumbled-up place in Wiltshire, where many things have come and gone—represents that moment of transition in which contrast is so vivid as to make it more dramatic than many plays—the very youngest throb of spring, with the brown slope of the foreground coming back to consciousness in pale lemon-colored patches and, on the top of the hill, against the still cold sky, the equally delicate forms of the wintry trees. By the time these forms have thickened, the expanses of daffodil will have become a mass of bluebells. All the daffodil pictures have a rare loveliness, but especially those that deal also with the earlier fruit-blossom, the young plum-trees in Berkshire orchards. Here the air is faintly pink, and the painter makes us feel the little *blow* in the thin blue sky. The spring, fortunately, is everybody's property and, in the language of all the arts, the easiest word to conjure with. It is therefore partly Mr. Parsons' good-luck that we enjoy so his rendering of these phases; but on the other hand we look twice when it's a case of meddling with the exquisite, and if he inspires us with respect it is because we feel that he has been deeply initiated. No one knows better the friendly reasons for our stopping, when chatting natives pronounce the weather "foine," at charming casual corners of old villages, where grassy ways cross each other and timbered houses bulge irregularly and there are fresh things behind crooked palings; witness the little vision of Blewbury, in Berkshire, reputedly of ancient British origin, with a road all round it and only footways within. No one, in the Herefordshire orchards, masses the white cow-parsley in such profusion under the apple blossoms; or makes the whitewashed little damson-trees look so innocently responsible and charming on the edge of the brook over which the planks are laid for the hens. Delightful, in this picture, is the sense of the clean spring day, after rain, with the blue of the sky washed faint. Delightful is the biggish view (one of the less numerous oil-pictures) of the Somersetshire garden, where that peculiarly English look of the open-air room is produced by the stretched carpet of the turf and the firm cushions of the hedges, and a pair of proprietors, perhaps happier than they know, are putting in an afternoon among their tulips, under the flushed apple-trees whose stems are so thin and whose brims so heavy. Are the absorbed couple, at any rate, aware of the surprising degree to which the clustered ruddy roofs of the next small town, over the hedge, off at the left, may remind the fanciful spectator of the way he has seen little dim Italian cities look on their hill-tops? The whole thing, in this subject, has the particular English note to which Mr. Parsons repeatedly testifies, the nook quality, the air of a land and a life so infinitely subdivided that they produce a thousand pleasant privacies. The painter moves with the months and finds, after the earliest things, the great bed of pansies in the angle of the old garden at Sutton, in which, for felicity of position and perfect pictorial service rendered—to say nothing of its polygonal, pyramidal roof—the ancient tool-house, or tea-house, is especially to be commended.

Very far descended is such a corner as this, very full of reference to vanished combinations and uses; and the artist communicates to us a feeling for it that makes us wish disinterstedly it may be still as long preserved.

He finds in June, at Blackdown, the blaze of the yellow azalea-bush, or in another spot the strong pink of the rhododendron, beneath the silver firs that deepen the blue of the sky. He finds the Vicarage Walk, at King's Langley, a smother of old-fashioned flowers—a midsummer vista for the figures of a happy lady and a lucky dog. He finds the delicious huddle of the gabled, pigeon-haunted roof of a certain brown old building at Frame, with poppies and gladiolus and hollyhock crowding the beautiful foreground. He finds— apparently in the same place—the tangle of the hardy flowers that come while the roses are still in bloom, with the tall blue larkspurs standing high among them. He finds the lilies, white and red, at Broadway, and the poppies, which have dropped most of their petals—apparently to let the roses, which are just coming out, give *their* grand party. Their humility is rewarded by the artist's admirable touch in the little bare poppy-heads that nod on their flexible pins.

But I cannot go on to say everything that such a seeker, such a discoverer, as Mr. Parsons finds—the less that the purpose of these limited remarks is to hint at our own *trouvailles*. A view of the field, at any rate, would be incomplete without such specimens as the three charming oil-pictures which commemorate Holme Lacey. There are gardens and gardens, and these represent the sort that are always spoken of in the plural and most arrogate the title. They form, in England, a magnificent collection, and if they abound in a quiet assumption of the grand style it must be owned that they frequently achieve it. There are people to be found who enjoy them, and it is not, at any rate, when Mr. Parsons deals with them that we have an opening for strictures. As we look at the blaze of full summer in the brilliantly conventional parterres we easily credit the tale of the 40,000 plants it takes to fill the beds. More than this, we like the long paths of turf that stretch between splendid borders, recalling the frescoed galleries of a palace; we like the immense hedges, whose tops are high against the sky. While we are liking, we like perhaps still better, since they deal with a very different order, the two water-colors from the dear little garden at Winchelsea—especially the one in which the lady takes he ease in her hammock (on a sociable, shady terrace, from which the ground drops), and looks at red Rye, across the marshes. Another garden where a contemplative hammock would be in order is the lovely canonical plot at Salisbury, with the everlasting spire above it tinted in the summer sky—unless, in the same place, you should choose to hook yourself up by the grassy bank of the Avon, at the end of the lawn, with the meadows, the cattle, the distant willows across the river, to look at.

Three admirable water-colors are devoted by Mr. Parsons to the perceptible dignity of Gravetye, in Sussex, the dignity of very serious gardens, entitled to ceremonious consideration, Few things in England can show a greater wealth of bloom than the wide flowery terrace immediately beneath the gray, gabled house, where tens of thousands of tea-roses, in predominant possession, have, in one direction, a mass of high yews for a background. They divide their province with the carnations and pansies: a wilder ness of tender petals ignorant of anything rougher than the neighborhood of the big unchanged medley of tall yuccas and saxifrage, with miscellaneous filling-in, in the picture which presents the charming house in profile. The artist shows us later, in September, at Gravetye, the pale violet multitude of the Michaelmas daisies; another I great bunch, or bank, of which half masks and greatly beautifies the rather bare yellow cottage at Broadway. This brings us on to the autumn, if I count as autumnal the admirable large water-color of a part of a garden at Shiplake, with the second bloom of the roses and a glimpse of a turn of the Thames. This exquisite picture expresses to perfection the beginning of the languor of the completed season—with its look of warm rest, of doing nothing, in the cloudless sky. To the same or a later moment belongs the straight walk at Fladbury—the old rectory garden by the Avon, with its Irish yews and the red lady in her chair; also the charming water-color of young, slim apple-trees, full of fruit (this must be October), beneath an admirable blue and white sky. Still later comes the big pear-tree that has turned, among barer boughs, to flame-color, and, in another picture, the very pale russet of the thinned cherry-trees, standing, beneath a grayish sky, above a foreshortened slope. Last of all we have, in oils, December and a hard frost in a bare apple-orchard, indented with a deep gully which makes the place somehow a subject and which, in fact, three or four years ago, made it one for a larger picture by Mr. Parsons, full of truth and style.

This completes his charming story of the life of the English year, told in a way that convinces us of his intimate acquaintance with it. Half the interest of Mr. Parsons' work is in the fact that he paints from a full mind and from a store of assimilated knowledge. In every touch of nature that he communicates to us we feel something of the thrill of the whole—we feel the innumerable relations, the possible variations of the particular objects. This makes his manner serious and masculine—rescues it from the thinness of tricks and the coquetries of *chic*. We walk with him on a firm earth, we taste the tone of the air and seem to take nature and the climate and all the complicated conditions by their big general hand. The painter's manner, in short, is one with the study of things—his talent is a part of their truth. In this happy series we seem to see still more how that talent was formed, how his rich motherland has been, from the earliest observation, its nurse and inspirer. He gives back to her all the good she has done him.

JOHN S. SARGENT

I was on the point of beginning this sketch of the work of an artist to whom distinction has come very early in life by saying, in regard to the degree to which the subject of it enjoys the attention of the public, that no American painter has hitherto won himself such recognition from the expert; but I find myself pausing at the start as on the edge of a possible solecism. Is Mr. Sargent in very fact an American painter? The proper answer to such a question is doubtless that we shall be well advised to pretend it, and the reason of this is simply that we have an excellent opportunity. Born in Europe, he has also spent his life in Europe, but none the less the burden of proof would rest with those who should undertake to show that he is a European. Moreover he has even on the face of it this great symptom of an American origin, that in the line of his art he might easily be mistaken for a Frenchman. It sounds like a paradox, but it is a very simple truth, that when to-day we look for "American art" we find it mainly in Paris. When we find it out of Paris, we at least find a great deal of Paris in it. Mr. Sargent came up to the irresistible city in his twentieth year, from Florence, where in 1856 he had been born of American parents and where his fortunate youth had been spent. He entered immediately the studio of Caro-lus Duran, and revealed himself in 1877, at the age of twenty-two, in the portrait of that master—-a fine model in more than one sense of the word. He was already in possession of a style; and if this style has gained both in finish and in assurance, it has not otherwise varied. As he saw and "rendered" ten years ago, so he sees and renders to-day; and I may add that there is no present symptom of his passing into another manner.

Those who have appreciated his work most up to the present time articulate no wish for a change, so completely does that work seem to them, in its kind, the exact translation of his thought, the exact "fit" of his artistic temperament. It is difficult to imagine a young painter less in the dark about his own ideal, more lucid and more responsible from the first about what he desires. In an altogether exceptional degree does he give us the sense that the intention and the art of carrying it out are for him one and the same thing. In the brilliant portrait of Carolus Duran, which he was speedily and strikingly to surpass, he gave almost the full measure of this admirable peculiarity, that perception with him is already by itself a kind of execution. It is likewise so, of course, with many another genuine painter; but in Sargent's case the process by which the object seen resolves itself into the object pictured is extraordinarily immediate. It is as if painting were pure tact of vision, a simple manner of feeling.

From the time of his first successes at the Salon he was hailed, I believe, as a recruit of high value to the camp of the Impressionists, and to-day he is for many people most conveniently pigeon-holed under that head. It is not necessary to protest against the classification if this addition always be made to it, that Mr. Sargent's impressions happen to be worthy of record. This is by no means inveterately the case with those of the ingenuous artists who most rejoice in the title in question. To render the impression of an object may be a very fruitful effort, but it is not necessarily so; that will depend upon what, I won't say the object, but the impression, may have been. The talents engaged in this school lie, not unjustly, as it seems to me under the suspicion of seeking the solution of their problem exclusively in simplification. If a painter works for other eyes as well as his own he courts a certain danger in this direction—that of being arrested by the cry of the spectator: "Ah! but excuse me; I myself take more impressions than that" We feel a synthesis not to be an injustice only when it is rich. Mr. Sargent simplifies, I think, but he simplifies with style, and his impression is the finest form of his energy.

His work has been almost exclusively in portraiture, and it has been his fortune to paint more women than men; therefore he has had but a limited opportunity to reproduce that generalized grand air with which his view of certain figures of gentlemen invests the model, which is conspicuous in the portrait of Carolus Duran and of which his splendid "Docteur Pozzi," the distinguished Paris surgeon (a work not sent to the Salon), is an admirable example. In each of these cases the model has been of a gallant pictorial type, one of the types which strike us as made for portraiture (which is by no means the way of all), as especially appears, for instance, in the handsome hands and frilled wrists of M. Carolus, whose cane rests in his fine fingers as if it were the hilt of a rapier. The most brilliant of all Mr. Sargent's productions is the portrait of a young lady, the magnificent picture which he exhibited in 1881; and if it has mainly been his fortune since to commemorate the fair faces of women, there is no ground for surprise at this sort of success on the part of one who had given so signal a proof of possessing the secret of the particular aspect that the contemporary lady (of any period) likes to wear in the eyes of posterity. Painted when he was but four-and-twenty years of age, the picture by which Mr. Sargent was represented at the Salon of 1881 is a performance which may well have made any critic of imagination rather anxious about his future. In common with the superb group of the children of Mr. Edward Boit, exhibited two years later, it offers the slightly "uncanny" spectacle of a talent which on the very threshold of its career has nothing more to learn. It is not simply precocity in the guise of maturity—a phenomenon we very often meet, which deceives us only for an hour; it is the freshness of youth combined with the artistic experience, really felt and assimilated, of generations. My admiration for this deeply distinguished work is such that I am perhaps in danger of overstating its merits; but it is worth taking into account that to-day, after several years' acquaintance with them, these merits seem to me more and more to justify enthusiasm. The picture has this sign of productions of the first order, that its style clearly would save it if everything else should change—our measure of its value of resemblance, its expression of character, the fashion of dress, the particular associations it evokes. It is not only a portrait, but a picture, and it arouses even in the profane spectator something of the painter's sense, the joy of engaging also, by sympathy, in the solution of the artistic problem. There are works of which it is sometimes said that they are painters' pictures (this description is apt to be intended invidiously), and the production of which I speak has the good-fortune at once to belong to this class and to give the "plain man" the kind of pleasure that the plain man looks for.

The young lady, dressed in black satin, stands upright, with her right hand bent back, resting on her waist, while the other, with the arm somewhat extended, offers to view a single white flower. The dress. stretched at the hips over a sort of hoop, and ornamented in front, where it opens on a velvet petticoat with large satin bows, has an old-fashioned air, as if it had been worn by some demure princess who might have sat for Velasquez. The hair, of which the arrangement is odd and charming, is disposed in two or three large curls fastened at one side over the temple with a comb. Behind the figure is the vague faded sheen, exquisite in tone, of a silk curtain, light, undefined, and losing itself at the bottom. The face is young, candid and peculiar. Out of these few elements the artist has constructed a picture which it is impossible to forget, of which the most striking characteristic is its simplicity, and yet which overflows with perfection. Painted with extraordinary breadth and freedom, so that surface and texture are interpreted by the lightest hand, it glows with life, character and distinction, and strikes us as the most complete—with one exception perhaps—of the author's productions. I know not why this representation of a young girl in black, engaged in the casual gesture of holding up a flower, should make so ineffaceable an impression and tempt one to become almost lyrical in its praise; but I remember that, encountering the picture unexpectedly in New York a year or two after it had been exhibited in Paris, it seemed to me to have acquired an extraordinary general value, to stand for more artistic truth than it would be easy to formulate. The language of painting, the tongue in which, exclusively, Mr. Sargent expresses himself, is a medium into which a considerable part of the public, for the simple an excellent reason that they don't understand it, will doubtless always be reluctant and unable to follow him.

Two years before he exhibited the young lady in black, in 1879, Mr. Sargent had spent several months in Spain, and here, even more than he had already been, the great Velasquez became the god of his idolatry. No scenes are more delightful to the imagination than those in which we figure youth and genius confronted with great examples, and if such matters did not belong to the domain of private life we might entertain ourselves with reconstructing the episode of the first visit to the museum of Madrid, the shrine of the painter of Philip IV., of a young Franco-American worshipper of the highest artistic sensibility, expecting a supreme revelation and prepared to fall on his knees. It is evident that Mr. Sargent fell on his knees and that in this attitude he passed a considerable part of his sojourn in Spain. He is various and experimental; if I am not mistaken, he sees each work that he produces in a light of its own, not turning off successive portraits according to some well-tried receipt which has proved useful in the case of their predecessors; nevertheless there is one idea that pervades them all, in a different degree, and gives them a family resemblance—the idea that it would be inspiring to know just how Velasquez would have treated the theme. We can fancy that on each occasion Mr. Sargent, as a solemn preliminary, invokes him as a patron saint. This is not, in my intention, tantamount to saying that the large canvas representing the contortions of a dancer in the lamp-lit room of a *posada*, which he exhibited on his return from Spain, strikes me as having come into the world under the same star as those compositions of the great Spaniard which at Madrid alternate with his royal portraits. This singular work, which has found an appreciative home in Boston, has the stamp of an extraordinary energy and facility—of an actual scene, with its accidents and peculiarities caught, as distinguished from a composition where arrangement and invention have played their part. It looks like life, but it looks also, to my view, rather like a perversion of life, and has the quality of an enormous "note" or memorandum, rather than of a representation. A woman in a voluminous white silk dress and a black mantilla pirouettes in the middle of a dusky room, to the accompaniment of her own castanets and that of a row of men and women who sit in straw chairs against the whitewashed wall and thrum upon guitar and tambourine or lift other castanets into the air. She appears almost colossal, and the twisted and inflated folds of her long dress increase her volume. She simpers, in profile, with a long chin, while she slants back at a dangerous angle, and the lamplight (it proceeds from below, as if she were on a big platform) makes a strange play in her large face. In the background the straight line of black-clad, black-hatted, white-shirted musicians projects shadows against the wall, on which placards, guitars, and dirty finger-marks display themselves. The merit of this production is that the air of reality is given in it with remarkable breadth and boldness; its defect it is difficult to express save by saying that it makes the spectator vaguely uneasy and even unhappy—an accident the more to be regretted as a lithe, inspired female figure, given up to the emotion of the dance, is not intrinsically a displeasing object. "El Jaleo" sins, in my opinion, in the direction of ugliness, and, independently of the fact that the heroine is circling round incommoded by her petticoats, has a want of serenity.

This is not the defect of the charming, dusky, white-robed person who, in the Tangerine subject exhibited at the Salon of 1880 (the fruit of an excursion to the African coast at the time of the artist's visit to Spain), stands on a rug, under a great white Moorish arch, and from out of the shadows of the large drapery, raised pentwise by her hands, which covers her head, looks down, with painted eyes and brows showing above a bandaged mouth, at the fumes of a beautiful censer or chafing-dish placed on the carpet. I know not who this stately Mahometan may be, nor in what mysterious domestic or religious rite she may be engaged; but in her muffled contemplation and her pearl-colored robes, under her plastered arcade which shines in the Eastern light, she transports and torments us. The picture is exquisite, a radiant effect of white upon white, of similar but discriminated tones. In dividing the honor that Mr. Sargent has won by his finest work between the portrait of the young lady of 1881 and the group of four little girls which was painted in 1882 and exhibited with the success it deserved the following year, I must be careful to give the latter picture not too small a share. The artist has done nothing more felicitous and interesting than this view of a rich dim, rather generalized French interior (the perspective of a hall with a shining floor, where screens and tall Japanese vases shimmer and loom), which encloses the life and seems to form the happy play-world of a family of charming children. The treatment is eminently unconventional, and there is none of the usual symmetrical balancing of the figures in the foreground. The place is regarded as a whole; it is a scene, a comprehensive impression; yet none the less do the little figures in their white pinafores (when was the pinafore ever painted with that power and made so poetic?) detach themselves and live with a personal life. Two of the sisters stand hand in hand at the back, in the delightful, the almost equal, company of a pair of immensely tall emblazoned jars, which overtop them and seem also to partake of the life of the picture; the splendid porcelain and the aprons of the children shine together, while a mirror in the brown depth behind them catches the light. Another little girl presents herself, with abundant tresses and slim legs, her hands behind her, quite to the left; and the youngest, nearest to the spectator, sits on the floor and plays with her doll. The naturalness of the composition, the loveliness of the complete effect, the light, free' security of the execution, the sense it gives us as of assimilated secrets and of instinct and knowledge playing together—all this makes the picture as astonishing a work on the part of a young man of twenty-six as the portrait of 1881 was astonishing on the part of a young man of twenty-four.

It is these remarkable encounters that justify us in writing almost prematurely of a career which is not yet half unfolded. Mr. Sargent is sometimes accused of a want of "finish," but if finish means the last word of expressiveness of touch, "The Hall with the Four Children," as we may call it, may-stand as a permanent reference on this point. If the picture of the Spanish dancer illustrates, as it seems to me to do, the latent dangers of the Impressionist practice, so this finer performance shows what victories it may achieve. And in relation to the latter I must repeat what I said about the young lady with the flower, that this is the sort of work which, when produced in youth, leads the attentive spectator to ask unanswerable questions. He finds himself murmuring, "Yes, but what is left?" and even wondering whether it be an advantage to an artist to obtain early in life such possession of his means that the struggle with them, discipline, *tâtonnement*, cease to exist for him. May not this breed an irresponsibility of cleverness, a wantonness, an irreverence—what is vulgarly termed a "larkiness"—on the part of the youthful genius who has, as it were, all his fortune in his pocket? Such are the possibly superfluous broodings of those who are critical even in their warmest admirations and who sometimes suspect that it may be better for an artist to have a certain part of his property invested in unsolved difficulties. When this is not the case, the question with regard to his future simplifies itself somewhat portentously. "What will he do with it?" we ask, meaning by the pronoun the sharp, completely forged weapon. It becomes more purely a question of responsibility, and we hold him altogether to a higher account. This is the case with Mr. Sargent; he knows so much about the art of painting that he perhaps does not fear emergencies quite enough, and that having knowledge to spare he may be tempted to play with it and waste it. Various, curious, as we have called him, he occasionally tries experiments which seem to arise from the mere high spirits of his brush, and runs risks little courted by the votaries of the literal, who never expose their necks to escape from the common. For the literal and the common he has the smallest taste; when he renders an object into the language of painting his translation is a generous paraphrase.

As I have intimated, he has painted little but portraits; but he has painted very many of these, and I shall not attempt in so few pages to give a catalogue of his works. Every canvas that has come from his hands has not figured at the Salon; some of them have seen the light at other exhibitions in Paris; some of them in London (of which city Mr. Sargent is now an inhabitant), at the Royal Academy and the Grosvenor Gallery. If he has been mainly represented by portraits there are two or three little subject-pictures of which I retain a grateful memory. There stands out in particular, as a pure gem, a small picture exhibited at the Grosvenor, representing a small group of Venetian girls of the lower class, sitting in gossip together one summer's day in the big, dim hall of a shabby old palazzo. The shutters let in a clink of light; the scagliola pavement gleams faintly in it; the whole place is bathed in a kind of transparent shade. The girls are vaguely engaged in some very humble household work; they are counting turnips or stringing onions, and these small vegetables, enchantingly painted, look as valuable as magnified pearls. The figures are extraordinarily natural and vivid; wonderfully light and fine is the touch by which the painter evokes the small familiar Venetian realities (he has handled them with a vigor altogether peculiar in various other studies which I have not space to enumerate), and keeps the whole thing free from that element of humbug which has ever attended most attempts to reproduce the idiosyncrasies of Italy. I am, however, drawing to the end of my remarks without having mentioned a dozen of those brilliant triumphs in the field of portraiture with which Mr. Sargent's name is preponderantly associated. I jumped from his "Carolus Duran" to the masterpiece of 1881 without speaking of the charming "Madame Pailleron" of 1879, or the picture of this lady's children the following year. Many, or rather most, of Mr. Sargent's sitters have been French, and he has studied the physiognomy of this nation so attentively that a little of it perhaps remains in the brush with which to-day, more than in his first years, he represents other types. I have alluded to his superb "Docteur Pozzi," to whose very handsome, still youthful head and slightly artificial posture he has given so fine a French cast that he might be excused if he should, even on remoter pretexts, find himself reverting to it. This gentleman stands up in his brilliant red dressing-gown with the *prestance* of a princely Vandyck. I should like to commemorate the portrait of a lady of a certain age and of an equally certain interest of appearance—a lady in black, with black hair, a black hat and a vast feather, which was displayed at that entertaining little annual exhibition of the "Mirlitons," in the Place Vendôme. With the exquisite modelling of its face (no one better than Mr. Sargent understands the beauty that resides in exceeding fineness), this head remains in my mind as a masterly rendering of the look of experience—such experience as may be attributed to a woman slightly faded and eminently distinguished. Subject and treatment in this valuable piece are of an equal interest, and in the latter there is an element of positive sympathy which is not always in a high degree the sign of Mr. Sargent's work. What shall I say of the remarkable canvas which, on the occasion of the Salon of 1884, brought the critics about our artist's ears, the already celebrated portrait of "Madame G.?" It is an experiment of a highly original kind, and the painter has had in the case, in regard to what Mr. Ruskin would call the "rightness" of his attempt, the courage of his opinion. A contestable beauty, according to Parisian fame, the lady stands upright beside a table on which her right arm rests, with her body almost fronting the spectator and her face in complete profile. She wears an entirely sleeveless dress of black satin, against which her admirable left arm detaches itself; the line of her harmonious profile has a sharpness which Mr. Sargent does not always seek, and the crescent of Diana, an ornament in diamonds, rests on her singular head. This work had not the good-fortune to please the public at large, and I believe it even excited a kind of unreasoned scandal—an idea sufficiently amusing in the light of some of the manifestations of the plastic effort to which, each year, the Salon stands sponsor. This superb picture, noble in conception and masterly in line, gives to the figure represented something of the high relief of the profiled images on great friezes. It is a work to take or to leave, as the phrase is, and one in regard to which the question of liking or disliking comes promptly to be settled. The author has never gone further in being boldly and consistently himself.

Two of Mr. Sargent's recent productions have been portraits of American ladies whom it must have been a delight to paint; I allude to those of Lady

Playfair and Mrs. Henry White, both of which were seen in the Royal Academy of 1885, and the former subsequently in Boston, where it abides. These things possess, largely, the quality which makes Mr. Sargent so happy as a painter of women—a quality which can best be expressed by a reference to what it is not, to the curiously literal, prosaic, sexless treatment to which, in the commonplace work that looks down at us from the walls of almost all exhibitions, delicate feminine elements have evidently so often been sacrificed. Mr. Sargent handles these elements with a special feeling for them, and they borrow a kind of noble intensity from his brush. This intensity is not absent from the two portraits I just mentioned, that of Lady Playfair and that of Mrs. Henry White; it looks out at us from the erect head and frank animation of the one, and the silvery sheen and shimmer of white satin and white lace which form the setting of the slim tall-ness of the other. In the Royal Academy of 1886 Mr. Sargent was represented by three important canvases, all of which reminded the spectator of how much the brilliant effect he produces in an English exhibition arises from a certain appearance that he has of looking down from a height, a height of cleverness, a sensible giddiness of facility, at the artistic problems of the given case. Sometimes there is even a slight impertinence in it; that, doubtless, was the impression of many of the people who passed, staring, with an ejaculation, before the triumphant group of the three Misses V. These young ladies, seated in a row, with a room much foreshortened for a background, and treated with a certain familiarity of frankness, excited in London a chorus of murmurs not dissimilar to that which it had been the fortune of the portrait exhibited in 1884 to elicit in Paris, and had the further privilege of drawing forth some prodigies of purblind criticism. Works of this character are a genuine service; after the short-lived gibes of the profane have subsided, they are found to have cleared the air. They remind people that the faculty of taking a direct, independent, unborrowed impression is not altogether lost.

In this very rapid review I have accompanied Mr. Sargent to a very recent date. If I have said that observers encumbered with a nervous temperament may at any moment have been anxious about his future, I have it on my conscience to add that the day has not yet come for a complete extinction of this anxiety. Mr. Sargent is so young, in spite of the place allotted to him in these pages, so often a record of long careers and uncontested triumphs that, in spite also of the admirable works he has already produced, his future is the most valuable thing he has to show. We may still ask ourselves what he will do with it, while we indulge the hope that he will see fit to give successors to the two pictures which I have spoken of emphatically as his finest. There is no greater work of art than a great portrait—a truth to be constantly taken to heart by a painter holding in his hands the weapon that Mr. Sargent wields. The gift that he possesses he possesses completely—the immediate perception of the end and of the means. Putting aside the question of the subject (and to a great portrait a common sitter will doubtless not always contribute), the highest result is achieved when to this element of quick perception a certain faculty of brooding reflection is added. I use this name for want of a better, and I mean the quality in the light of which the artist sees deep into his subject, undergoes it, absorbs it, discovers in it new things that were not on the surface, becomes patient with it, and almost reverent, and, in short, enlarges and humanizes the technical problem.

HONORÉ DAUMIER

AS we attempt, at the present day, to write the history of everything, it would be strange if we had happened to neglect the annals of caricature; for the very essence of the art of Cruikshank and Gavarni, of Daumier and Leech, is to be historical; and every one knows how addicted is this great science to discoursing about itself. Many industrious seekers, in England and France, have ascended the stream of time to the source of the modern movement of pictorial satire. The stream of time is in this case mainly the stream of journalism; for social and political caricature, as the present century has practised it, is only journalism made doubly vivid.

The subject indeed is a large one, if we reflect upon it, for many people would tell us that journalism is the greatest invention of our age. If this rich affluent has shared the great fortune of the general torrent, so, on other sides, it touches the fine arts, touches manners, touches morals. All this helps to account for its inexhaustible life; journalism is the criticism of the moment *at* the moment, and caricature is that criticism at once simplified and intensified by a plastic form. We know the satiric image as periodical, and above all as punctual—the characteristics of the printed sheet with which custom has at last inveterately associated it.

This, by-the-way, makes us wonder considerably at the failure of caricature to achieve, as yet, a high destiny in America—a failure which might supply an occasion for much explanatory discourse, much searching of the relations of things. The newspaper has been taught to flourish among us as it flourishes nowhere else, and to flourish moreover on a humorous and irreverent basis; yet it has never taken to itself this helpful concomitant of an unscrupulous spirit and a quick periodicity. The explanation is probably that it needs an old society to produce ripe caricature. The newspaper thrives in the United States, but journalism languishes; for the lively propagation of news is one thing and the large interpretation of it is another. A society has to be old before it becomes critical, and it has to become critical before it can take pleasure in the reproduction of its incongruities by an instrument as impertinent as the indefatigable crayon. Irony, scepticism, pessimism are, in any particular soil, plants of gradual growth, and it is in the art of caricature that they flower most aggressively. Furthermore they must be watered by education—I mean by the education of the eye and hand—all of which things take time. The soil must be rich too, the incongruities must swarm. It is open to doubt whether a pure democracy is very liable to make this particular satiric return upon itself; for which it would seem tha' certain social complications are indispensable. These complications are supplied from the moment a democracy becomes, as we may say, impure from its own point of view; from the moment variations and heresies, deviations or perhaps simple affirmations of taste and temper begin to multiply within it. Such things afford a *point d'appui*; for it is evidently of the essence of caricature to be reactionary. We hasten to add that its satiric force varies immensely in kind and in degree according to the race, or to the individual talent, that takes advantage of it.

I used just now the term pessimism; but that was doubtless in a great measure because I have been turning over a collection of the extraordinarily vivid drawings of Honoré Daumier. The same impression would remain with me, no doubt, if I had been consulting an equal quantity of the work of Gavarni the wittiest, the most literary and most acutely profane of all chartered mockers with the pencil. The feeling of disrespect abides in all these things, the expression of the spirit for which humanity is definable primarily by its weaknesses. For Daumier these weaknesses are altogether ugly and grotesque, while for Gavarni they are either basely graceful or touchingly miserable; but the vision of them in both cases is close and direct. If, on the other hand, we look through a dozen volumes of the collection of *Punch* we get an equal impression of hilarity, but we by no means get an equal impression of irony. Certainly the pages of *Punch* do not reek with pessimism; their "criticism of life" is gentle and forbearing. Leech is positively optimistic; there is at any rate nothing infinite in his irreverence; it touches bottom as soon as it approaches the pretty woman or the nice girl. It is such an apparition as this that really, in Gavarni, awakes the scoffer. Du Maurier is as graceful as Gavarni, but his sense of beauty conjures away almost everything save our

67

minor vices. It is in the exploration of our major ones that Gavarni makes his principal discoveries of charm or of absurdity of attitude. None the less, of course, the general inspiration of both artists is the same: the desire to try the innumerable different ways in which the human subject may *not* be taken seriously.

If this view of that subject, in its plastic manifestations, makes history of a sort, it will not in general be of a kind to convert those persons who find history sad reading. The writer of the present lines remained unconverted, lately, on an occasion on which many cheerful influences were mingled with his impression. They were of a nature to which he usually does full justice, even overestimating perhaps their charm of suggestion; but, at the hour I speak of, the old Parisian quay, the belittered print-shop, the pleasant afternoon, the glimpse of the great Louvre on the other side of the Seine, in the interstices of the sallow *estampes* suspended in window and doorway— all these elements of a rich actuality availed only to mitigate, without transmuting, that general vision of a high, cruel pillory which pieced itself together as I drew specimen after specimen from musty portfolios. I had been passing the shop when I noticed in a small *vitrine*, let into the embrasure of the doorway, half a dozen soiled, striking lithographs, which it took no more than a first glance to recognize as the work of Daumier. They were only old pages of the *Charivari*, torn away from the text and rescued from the injury of time; and they were accompanied with an inscription to the effect that many similar examples of the artist were to be seen within. To become aware of this circumstance was to enter the shop and to find myself promptly surrounded with bulging; *cartons* and tattered relics. These relics—crumpled leaves of the old comic journals of the period from 1830 to 1855—are neither rare nor expensive; but I happened to have lighted on a particularly copious collection, and I made the most of my small good-fortune, in order to transmute it, if possible, into a sort of compensation for my having missed unavoidably, a few months before, the curious exhibition "de la Caricature Moderne" held for several weeks just at hand, in the École des Beaux-Arts.

Daumier was said to have appeared there in considerable force; and it was a loss not to have had that particular opportunity of filling one's mind with him.

There was perhaps a perversity in having wished to do so, strange, indigestible stuff of contemplation as he might appear to be; but the perversity had had an honorable growth. Daumier's great days were in the reign of Louis-Philippe; but in the early years of the Second Empire he still plied his coarse and formidable pencil. I recalled, from a juvenile consciousness, the last failing strokes of it. They used to impress me in Paris, as a child, with their abnormal blackness as well as with their grotesque, magnifying movement, and there was something in them that rather scared a very immature admirer. This small personage, however, was able to perceive later, when he was unfortunately deprived of the chance of studying them, that there were various things in them besides the power to excite a vague alarm. Daumier was perhaps a great artist; at all events unsatisfied curiosity increased in proportion to that possibility.

The first complete satisfaction of it was really in the long hours that I spent in the little shop on the quay. There I filled my mind with him, and there too, at no great cost, I could make a big parcel of these cheap reproductions of his work. This work had been shown in the Ecole des Beaux-Arts as it came from his hand; M. Champfleury, his biographer, his cataloguer and devotee, having poured forth the treasures of a precious collection, as I suppose they would be called in the case of an artist of higher flights. It was only as he was seen by the readers of the comic journals of his day that I could now see him; but I tried to make up for my want of privilege by prolonged immersion. I was not able to take home all the portfolios from the shop on the quay, but I took home what I could, and I went again to turn over the superannuated piles. I liked looking at them on the spot; I seemed still surrounded by the artist's vanished Paris and his extinct Parisians. Indeed no quarter of the delightful city probably shows, on the whole, fewer changes from the aspect it wore during the period of Louis-Philippe, the time when it will ever appear to many of its friends to have been most delightful. The long line of the quay is unaltered, and the rare charm of the river. People came and went in the shop: it is a wonder how many, in the course of an hour, may lift the latch even of an establishment that pretends to no great business. What was all this small, sociable, contentious life but the great Daumier's subject-matter? He was the painter of the Parisian bourgeois, and the voice of the bourgeois was in the air.

M. Champfleury has given a summary of Daumier's career in his smart little *Histoire e la Caricature Moderne*, a record not at all abundant in personal detail. The biographer has told his story better perhaps in his careful catalogue of the artist's productions, the first sketch of which is to be found in *L'Art* for 1878. This copious list is Daumier's real history; his life cannot have been a very different business from his work. I read in the interesting publication of M. Grand-Carteret (*Les Moeurs et la Caricature en France* 1888) that our artist produced nearly 4000 lithographs and a thousand drawings on wood, up to the time when failure of eyesight compelled him to rest. This is not the sort of activity that leaves a man much time for independent adventures, and Daumier was essentially of the type, common in France, of the specialist so immersed in his specialty that he can be painted in only one attitude—a general circumstance which perhaps helps to account for the paucity, in that country, of biography, in our English sense of the word, in proportion to the superabundance of criticism.

Honoré Daumier was born at Marseilles February 26th, 1808; he died on the 11th of the same month, 1879. His main activity, however, was confined to the earlier portion of a career of almost exactly seventy-one years, and I find it affirmed in Vapereau's *Dictionnaire des Contemporains* that he became completely blind between 1850 and 1860. He enjoyed a pension from the State of 2400 francs; but what relief from misery could mitigate a quarter of a century of darkness for a man who had looked out at the world with such vivifying eyes? His father had followed the trade of a glazier, but was otherwise vocal than in the emission of the rich street-cry with which we used all to be familiar, and which has vanished with so many other friendly pedestrian notes. The elder Daumier wrought verses as well as window-panes, and M. Champfleury has disinterred a small volume published by him in 1823. The merit of his poetry is not striking; but he was able to transmit the artistic nature to his son, who, becoming promptly conscious of it, made the inevitable journey to Paris in search of fortune.

The young draughtsman appeared to have missed at first the way to this boon; inasmuch as in the year 1832 he found himself condemned to six months' imprisonment for a lithograph disrespectful to Louis-Philippe. This drawing had appeared in the *Caricature*, an organ of pictorial satire founded in those days by one Philipon, with the aid of a band of young mockers to whom he gave ideas and a direction, and several others, of whom Gavarni, Henry Monnier, Decamps, Grandville, were destined to make themselves a place. M. Eugène Montrosier, in a highly appreciative article on Daumier in *L'Art* for 1878, says that this same Philipon was *le journalisme fait homme*; which did not prevent him—rather in fact fostered such a result—from being perpetually in delicate relations with the government. He had had many horses killed under him, and had led a life of attacks, penalties, suppressions and resurrections. He subsequently established the *Charivari* and launched a publication entitled *L'Association Lithographique Mensuelle*, which brought to light much of Daumier's early work. The artist passed rapidly from seeking his way to finding it, and from an ineffectual to a vigorous form.

In this limited compass and in the case of such a quantity of production it is almost impossible to specify—difficult to pick dozens of examples out of thousands. Daumier became more and more the political spirit of the *Charivari*, or at least the political pencil, for M. Philipon, the breath of whose nostrils was opposition—one perceives from here the little bilious, bristling, ingenious, insistent man—is to be credited with a suggestive share in any enterprise in which he had a hand. This pencil played over public life, over the sovereign, the ministers, the deputies, the peers, the judiciary, the men and the measures, the reputations and scandals of the moment, with a strange, ugly, extravagant, but none the less sane and manly vigor. Daumier's sign is strength above all, and in turning over his pages to-day there is no intensity of force that the careful observer will not concede to him. It is perhaps another matter to assent to the proposition, put forth by his greatest admirers among his countrymen, that he is the first of all caricaturists. To the writer of this imperfect sketch he remains considerably less interesting than Gavarni; and/or a particular reason, which it is difficult to express otherwise than by saying that he is too simple. Simplicity was not Gavarni's fault, and indeed to a large degree it was Daumier's merit. The single grossly ridiculous or almost hauntingly characteristic thing which his figures represent is largely the reason why they still represent life and an unlucky reality years after the names attached to them have parted with a vivifying power. Such vagueness has overtaken them, for the most part, and to such a thin reverberation have they shrunk, the persons and the affairs which were then so intensely sketchable. Daumier handled them with a want of ceremony which would have been brutal were it not for the element of science in his work, making them immense and unmistakable in their drollery, or at least in their grotesqueness; for the term drollery suggests gayety, and Daumier is anything but gay. *Un rude peintre de moeurs*, M. Champfleury calls him; and the phrase expresses his extreme breadth of treatment.

Of the victims of his "rudeness" M. Thiers is almost the only one whom the present generation may recognize without a good deal of reminding, and indeed his hand is relatively light in delineating this personage of few inches and many episodes. M. Thiers must have been dear to the caricaturist, for he belonged to the type that was easy to "do;" it being well known that these gentlemen appreciate public characters in direct proportion to their saliency of feature. When faces are reducible to a few telling strokes their wearers are overwhelmed with the honors of publicity; with which, on the other hand, nothing is more likely to interfere than the possession of a countenance neatly classical. Daumier had only to give M. Thiers the face of a clever owl, and the trick was played. Of course skill was needed to individualize the symbol, but that is what caricaturists propose to themselves. Of how well he succeeded the admirable plate of the lively little minister in a "new dress"—tricked out in the uniform of a general of the First Republic—is a sufficient illustration. The bird of night is not an acute bird, but how the artist has presented the image of a selected specimen! And with what a life-giving pencil the whole figure is put on its feet, what intelligent drawing, what a rich, free stroke! The allusions conveyed in it are to such forgotten things that it is strange to think the personage was, only the other year, still contemporaneous; that he might have been met, on a fine day, taking a few firm steps in a quiet part of the Champs Élysées, with his footman carrying a second overcoat and looking doubly tall behind him. In whatever attitude Daumier depicts him, planted as a tiny boxing-master at the feet of the virtuous colossus in a blouse (whose legs are apart, like those-of the Rhodian), in whom the artist represents the People, to watch the match that is about to come off between Ratapoil and M. Berryer, or even in the act of lifting the "parricidal" club of a new repressive law to deal a blow at the Press, an effulgent, diligent, sedentary muse (this picture, by the way, is a perfect specimen of the simple and telling in political caricature)—however, as I say, he takes M. Thiers, there is always a rough indulgence in his crayon, as if he were grateful to him for lending himself so well. He invented Ratapoil as he appropriated Robert Macaire, and as a caricaturist he never fails to put into circulation, when he can, a character to whom he may attribute as many as possible of the affectations or the vices of the day. Robert Macaire, an imaginative, a romantic rascal, was the hero of a highly successful melodrama written for Frederick Lemaitre; but Daumier made him the type of the swindler at large in an age of feverish speculation—the projector of showy companies, the advertiser of worthless shares. There is a whole series of drawings descriptive of his exploits, a hundred masterly plates which, according to M. Champfleury, consecrated Daumier's reputation. The subject, the legend, was in most cases, still according to M. Champfleury, suggested by Philipon. Sometimes it was very witty; as for instance when Bertrand, the muddled acolyte or scraping second fiddle of the hero, objects, in relation to a brilliant scheme which he has just developed, with the part Bertrand is to play, that there are constables in the country, and he promptly replies, "Constables? So much the better—they'll take the shares!" Ratapoil was an evocation of the same general character, but with a difference of *nuance*—the ragged political bully, or hand-to-mouth demagogue, with the smashed tall hat, cocked to one side, the absence of linen, the club half-way up his sleeve, the swagger and pose of being gallant for the people. Ratapoil abounds in the promiscuous drawings that I have looked over, and is always very strong and living, with a considerable element of the sinister, so often in Daumier an accompaniment of the comic. There is an admirable page—it brings the idea down to 1851—in which a sordid but astute peasant, twirling his thumbs on his stomach and looking askance, allows this political adviser to urge upon him in a whisper that there is not a minute to lose—to lose for action, of course—if he wishes to keep his wife, his house, his field, his heifer and his calf. The canny scepticism in the ugly, half-averted face of the typical rustic who considerably suspects his counsellor is indicated by a few masterly strokes.

This is what the student of Daumier recognizes as his science, or, if the word has a better grace, his art. It is what has kept life in his work so long after so many of the occasions of it have been swept into darkness. Indeed, there is no such commentary on renown as the "back numbers" of a comic journal. They show us that at certain moments certain people were eminent, only to make us unsuccessfully try to remember what they were eminent *for*. And the comparative obscurity (comparative, I mean, to the talent of the caricaturist) overtakes even the most justly honored names. M. Berryer was a splendid speaker and a public servant of real distinction and the highest utility; yet the fact that to-day his name is on few men's lips seems to be emphasized by this other fact that we continue to pore over Daumier, in whose plates we happen to come across him. It reminds one afresh how Art is an embalmer, a magician, whom we can never speak too fair. People duly impressed with this truth are sometimes laughed at for their superstitious tone, which is pronounced, according to the fancy of the critic, mawkish, maudlin or hysterical. But it is really difficult to see how any reiteration of the importance of art can overstate the plain facts. It prolongs, it preserves, it consecrates, it raises from the dead. It conciliates, charms, bribes posterity; and it murmurs to mortals, as the old French poet sang to his mistress, "You will be fair only so far as I have said so." When it whispers even to the great, "You depend upon me, and I can do more for you, in the long-run, than any one else," it is scarcely too proud. It puts method and power and the strange, real, mingled air of things into Daumier's black sketchiness, so full of the technical *gras*, the "fat" which French critics commend and which we have no word to express. It puts power above all, and the effect which he best achieves, that of a certain simplification of the attitude or the gesture to an almost symbolic generality. His persons represent only one thing, but they insist tremendously on that, and their expression of it abides with us, unaccompanied with timid detail. It may really be said that they represent only one class—the old and ugly; so that there is proof enough of a special faculty in his having played such a concert, lugubrious though it be, on a single chord. It has been made a reproach to him, says M. Grand-Carteret, that "his work is lacking in two capital elements—*la jeunesse et la femme*;" and the commentator resents his being made to suffer for the deficiency—"as if an

74

artist could be at the same time deep, comic, graceful and pretty; as if all those who have a real value had not created for themselves a form to which they remain confined and a type which they reproduce in all its variations, as soon as they have touched the æsthetic ideal that has been their dream. Assuredly humanity, as this great painter saw it, could not be beautiful; one asks one's self what maiden in her teens, a pretty face, would have done in the midst of these good, plain folk, stunted and elderly, with faces like wrinkled apples. A simple accessory most of the time, woman is for him merely a termagant or a blue-stocking who has turned the corner."

When the eternal feminine, for Daumier appears in neither of these forms he sees it in Madame Chaboulard or Madame Fribochon, the old snuff-taking, gossiping portress, in a nightcap and shuffling *savates*, relating or drinking in the wonderful and the intimate. One of his masterpieces represents three of these dames, lighted by a guttering candle, holding their heads together to discuss the fearful earthquake at Bordeaux, the consequence of the government's allowing the surface of the globe to be unduly dug out in California. The representation of confidential imbecility could not go further. When a man leaves out so much of life as Daumier—youth and beauty and the charm of woman and the loveliness of childhood and the manners of those social groups of whom it may most be said that they *have* manners— when he exhibits a deficiency on this scale it might seem that the question was not to be so easily disposed of as in the very non-apologetic words I have just quoted. All the same (and I confess it is singular), we may feel what Daumier omitted and yet not be in the least shocked by the claim of predominance made for him. It is impossible to spend a couple of hours over him without assenting to this claim, even though there may be a weariness in such a panorama of ugliness and an inevitable reaction from it. This anomaly, and the challenge to explain it which appears to proceed from him, render him, to my sense, remarkably interesting. The artist whose idiosyncrasies, whose limitations, if you will, make us question and wonder, in the light of his fame, has an element of fascination not attaching to conciliatory talents. If M. Eugene Montrosier may say of him without scandalizing us that such and such of his drawings belong to the very highest art, it is interesting (and Daumier profits by the interest) to put one's finger on the reason we are not scandalized.

I think this reason is that, on the whole he is so peculiarly serious. This may seem an odd ground of praise for a jocose draughtsman, and of course what I mean is that his comic force is serious—a very different thin from the absence of comedy. This essential sign of the caricaturist may surely be anything it will so long as it is there. Daumier's figures are almost always either foolish, fatuous politicians or frightened, mystified bourgeois; yet they help him to give us a strong sense of the nature of man. They are some times so serious that they are almost tragic the look of the particular pretension, combined with inanity, is carried almost to madness. There is a magnificent drawing of the series of "Le Public du Salon," old classicists looking up, horrified and scandalized, at the new romantic work of 1830, in which the faces have an appalling gloom of mystification and platitude. We feel that Daumier reproduces admirably the particular life that he sees, because it is the very medium in which he moves. He has no wide horizon; the absolute bourgeois hems him in, and he is a bourgeois himself, without poetic ironies, to whom a big cracked mirror has been given. His thick, strong, manly touch stands, in every way, for so much knowledge. He used to make little images, in clay and in wax (many of them still exist), of the persons he was in the habit of representing, so that they might constantly seem to be "sitting" for him. The caricaturist of that day had not the help of the ubiquitous photograph. Daumier painted actively, as well, in his habitation, all dedicated to work, on the narrow island of St. Louis, where the Seine divides and where the monuments of old Paris stand thick, and the types that were to his purpose pressed close upon him. He had not far to go to encounter the worthy man, in the series of "Les Papas," who is reading the evening paper at the café with so amiable and placid a credulity, while his unnatural little boy, opposite to him, finds sufficient entertainment in the much-satirized *Constitutionnel*. The bland absorption of the papa, the face of the man who believes everything he sees in the newspaper, is as near as Daumier often comes to positive gentleness of humor. Of the same family is the poor gentleman, in "Actualités," seen, in profile, under a doorway where he has taken refuge from a torrent of rain, who looks down at his neat legs with a sort of speculative contrition and says, "To think of my having just ordered two pairs of white trousers." The *tout petit bourgeois* palpitates in both these sketches.

I must repeat that it is absurd to pick half a dozen at hazard, out of five thousand; yet a few selections are the only way to call attention to his strong drawing. This has a virtuosity of its own, for all its hit-or-miss appearance. Whatever he touches—the nude, in the swimming-baths on the Seine, the intimations of landscape, when his *petits rentiers* go into the suburbs for a Sunday—acquires relief and character, Docteur Véron, a celebrity of the reign of Louis-Philippe, a Mæcenas of the hour, a director of the opera, author of the *Mémoires d'un Bourgeois de Paris*—this temporary "illustration," who appears to have been almost indecently ugly, would not be vivid to us to-day had not Daumier, who was often effective at his expense, happened to have represented him, in some crisis of his career, as a sort of naked inconsolable Vitellius. He renders the human body with a cynical sense of its possible flabbiness and an intimate acquaintance with its structure. "Une Promenade Conjugale," in the series of "Tout ce qu'on voudra," portrays a hillside, on a summer afternoon, on which a man has thrown himself on his back to rest, with his arms locked under his head. His fat, full-bosomed, middle-aged wife, under her parasol, with a bunch of field-flowers in her hand, looks down at him patiently and seems to say, "Come, my dear, get up." There is surely no great point in this; the only point is life, the glimpse of the little snatch of poetry in prose. It is a matter of a few broad strokes of the crayon; yet the pleasant laziness of the man, the idleness of the day, the fragment of homely, familiar dialogue, the stretch of the field with a couple of trees merely suggested, have a communicative truth.

I perhaps exaggerate all this, and in insisting upon the merit of Daumier may appear to make light of the finer accomplishment of several more modern talents, in England and France, who have greater ingenuity and subtlety and have carried qualities of execution so, much further. In looking at this complicated younger work, which has profited so by experience and comparison, it is inevitable that we should perceive it to be infinitely more cunning. On the other hand Daumier, moving in his contracted circle, has an impressive depth. It comes back to his strange seriousness. He is a draughtsman by race, and if he has not extracted the same brilliancy from training, or perhaps even from effort and experiment, as some of his successors, does not his richer satiric and sympathetic feeling more than make up the difference?

However this question may be answered, some of his drawings belong to the class of the unforgetable. It may be a perversity of prejudice, but even the little cut of the "Connoisseurs," the group of gentlemen collected round a picture and criticising it in various attitudes of sapience and sufficiency, appears to me to have the strength that abides. The criminal in the dock, the flat-headed murderer, bending over to speak to his advocate, who turns a whiskered, professional, anxious head to caution and remind him. tells a large, terrible story and awakes a recurrent shudder. We see the gray court-room, we feel the personal suspense and the immensity of justice. The "Saltimbanques," reproduced in *L'Art* for 1878, is a page of tragedy, the finest of a cruel series. M. Eugène Montrosier says of it that "The drawing is masterly, incomparably firm, the composition superb, the general impression quite of the first order." It exhibits a pair of lean, hungry mountebanks, a clown and a harlequin beating the drum and trying a comic attitude to attract the crowd, at a fair, to a poor booth in front of which a painted canvas, offering to view a simpering fat woman, is suspended. But the crowd doesn't come, and the battered tumblers, with their furrowed cheeks, go through their pranks in the void. The whole thing is symbolic and full of grim-ness, imagination and pity. It is the sense that we shall find in him, mixed with his homelier extravagances, an element prolific in indications of this order that draws us back to Daumier.

AFTER THE PLAY

The play was not over when the curtain fell, four months ago; it was continued in a supplementary act or epilogue which took place immediately afterwards. "Come home to tea," Florentia said to certain friends who had stopped to speak to her in the lobby of the little theatre in Soho—they had been present at a day performance by the company of the Theatre Libre, transferred for a week from Paris; and three of these—Auberon and Dorriforth, accompanying Amicia—turned up so expeditiously that the change of scene had the effect of being neatly executed. The short afterpiece—it was in truth very slight—began with Amicia's entrance and her declaration that she would never again go to an afternoon performance: it was such a horrid relapse into the real to find it staring at you through the ugly daylight on coming out of the blessed fictive world.

Dorriforth. Ah, you touch there on one of the minor sorrows of life. That's an illustration of the general change that comes to pass in us as we grow older, if we have ever loved the stage: the fading of the glamour and the mystery that surround it.

Auberon. Do you call it a minor sorrow? It's one of the greatest. And nothing can mitigate it.

Amicia. Wouldn't it be mitigated a little if the stage were a trifle better? You must remember how that has changed.

Auberon. Never, never: it's the same old stage. The change is in ourselves.

Florentia. Well, I never would have given an evening to what we have just seen. If one could have put it in between luncheon and tea, well enough. But one's evenings are too precious.

Dorriforth. Note that—it's very important.

Florentia. I mean too precious for that sort of thing.

Auberon. Then you didn't sit spellbound by the little history of the Due d'Enghien?

Florentia. I sat yawning. Heavens, what a piece!

Amicia. Upon my word I liked it. The last act made me cry.

Dorriforth. Wasn't it a curious, interesting specimen of some of the things that are worth trying: an attempt to sail closer to the real?

Auberon. How much closer? The fiftieth part of a point—it isn't calculable.

Florentia. It was just like any other play—I saw no difference. It had neither a plot, nor a subject, nor dialogue, nor situations, nor scenery, nor costumes, nor acting.

Amicia. Then it was hardly, as you say, just like any other play.

Auberon. Florentia should have said like any other *bad* one. The only way it differed seemed to be that it was bad in theory as well as in fact.

Amicia. It's a *morceau de vie*, as the French say.

Auberon. Oh, don't begin on the French!

Amicia. It's a French experiment—*que voulez-vous?*

Auberon. English experiments will do.

Dorriforth. No doubt they would—if there *were* any. But I don't see them.

Amicia. Fortunately: think what some of them might be! Though Florentia saw nothing I saw many things in this poor little shabby "Due d'Enghien," coming over to our roaring London, where the dots have to be so big on the i's, with its barely audible note of originality. It appealed to me, touched me, offered me a poignant suggestion of the way things happen in life.

Auberon. In life they happen clumsily, stupidly, meanly. One goes to the theatre just for the refreshment of seeing them happen in another way—in symmetrical, satisfactory form, with unmistakable effect and just at the right moment.

Dorriforth. It shows how the same cause may produce the most diverse consequences. In this truth lies the only hope of art.

Auberon. Oh, art, art—don't talk about art!

Amicia. Mercy, we must talk about something!

Dorriforth. Auberon hates generalizations. Nevertheless I make bold to say that we go to the theatre in the same spirit in which we read a novel, some of us to find one thing and some to find another; and according as we look for the particular thing we find it.

Auberon. That's a profound remark.

Florentia. We go to find amusement: that, surely, is what we all go for.

Amicia. There's such a diversity in our idea of amusement.

Auberon. Don't you impute to people more ideas than they have?

Dorriforth. Ah, one must do that or one couldn't talk about them. We go to be interested; to be absorbed, beguiled and to lose ourselves, to give ourselves up, in short, to a charm.

Florentia. And the charm is the strange, the extraordinary.

Amicia. Ah, speak for yourself! The charm is the recognition of what we know, what we feel.

Dorriforth. See already how you differ.

"SO!"

What we surrender ourselves to is the touch of nature, the sense of life.

Amicia. The first thing is to believe.

Florentia. The first thing, on the contrary, is to *dis*believe.

Auberon. Lord, listen to them!

Dorriforth. The first thing is to folio—to care.

81

Florentia. I read a novel, I go to the theatre, to forget.

Amicia. To forget what?

Florentia. To forget life; to thro myself into something more beautiful more exciting: into fable and romance.

Dorriforth. The attraction of fable and romance is that it's about *us*, about you and me—or people whose power to suffer and to enjoy is the same as ours. In other words, we *live* their experience, for the time, and that's hardly escaping from life.

Florentia. I'm not at all particular as to what you call it. Call it an escape from the common, the prosaic, the immediate.

Dorriforth. You couldn't put it better. That's the life that art, with Auberon's permission, gives us; that's the distinction it confers. This is why the greatest commonness is when our guide turns out a vulgar fellow—the angel, as we had supposed him, who has taken us by the hand. Then what becomes of our escape?

Florentia. It's precisely then that I complain of him. He leads us into foul and dreary places—into flat and foolish deserts.

Dorriforth. He leads us into his own mind, his own vision of things: that's the only place into which the poet *can* lead us. It's there that he finds "As You Like It," it is there that he finds "Comus," or "The Way of the World," or the Christmas pantomime. It is when he betrays us, after he has got us in and locked the door, when he can't keep from us that we are in a bare little hole and that there are no pictures on the walls, it is then that the immediate and the foolish overwhelm us.

Amicia. That's what I liked in the piece we have been looking at. There was an artistic intention, and the little room wasn't bare: there was sociable company in it. The actors were very humble aspirants, they were common—

Auberon. Ah, when the French give their mind to that—!

Amicia. Nevertheless they struck me as recruits to an interesting cause, which as yet (the house was so empty) could confer neither money nor glory. They had the air, poor things, of working for love.

Auberon. For love of what?

Amicia. Of the whole little enterprise—the idea of the Théâtre Libre.

Florentia. Gracious, what you see in things! Don't you suppose they were paid?

Amicia. I know nothing about it. I liked their shabbiness—they had only what was indispensable in the way of dress and scenery. That often pleases me: the imagination, in certain cases, is more finely persuaded by the little than by the much.

Dorriforth. I see what Amicia means.

Florentia. I'll warrant you do, and a great deal more besides.

Dorriforth. When the appointments are meagre and sketchy the responsibility that rests upon the actors becomes a still more serious thing, and the spectator's observation of the way they rise to it a pleasure more intense. The face and the voice are more to the purpose than acres of painted canvas, and a touching intonation, a vivid gesture or two, than an army of supernumeraries.

Auberon. Why not have everything—the face, the voice, the touching intonations, the vivid gestures, the acres of painted canvas, *and* the army of supernumeraries? Why not use bravely and intelligently every resource of which the stage disposes? What else was Richard Wagner's great theory, in producing his operas at Bayreuth?

Dorriforth. Why not, indeed? That would be the ideal. To have the picture complete at the same time the figures do their part in producing the particular illusion required—what a perfection and what a joy! I know no answer to that save the aggressive, objectionable fact. Simply look at the stage of to-day and observe that these two branches of the matter never do happen to go together. There is evidently a corrosive principle in the large command of machinery and decorations—a germ of perversion and corruption. It gets the upperhand—it becomes the master. It is so much less easy to get good actors than good scenery and to represent a situation by the delicacy of personal art than by "building it in" and having everything real. Surely there is no reality worth a farthing, on the stage, but what the actor gives, and only when he has learned his business up to the hilt need he concern himself with his material accessories. He hasn't a decent respect for his art unless he be ready to render his part as if the whole illusion depended on that alone and the accessories didn't exist. The acting is everything or it's nothing. It ceases to be everything as soon as something else becomes very important. This is the case, to-day, on the London stage: something else is very important. The public have been taught to consider it so: the clever machinery has ended by operating as a bribe and a blind. Their sense of the rest of the matter has gone to the dogs, as you may perceive when you hear a couple of occupants of the stalls talking, in a tone that excites your curiosity, about a performance that's "splendid."

Amicia. Do you ever hear the occupants of the stalls talking? Never, in the *entr'actes*, have I detected, on their lips, a criticism or a comment.

Dorriforth. Oh, they say "splendid"—distinctly! But a question or two reveals that their reference is vague: they don't themselves know whether they mean the art of the actor or that of the stage-carpenter.

Auberon. Isn't that confusion a high result of taste? Isn't it what's called a feeling for the *ensemble?* The artistic effect, as a whole, is so welded together that you can't pick out the parts.

Dorriforth. Precisely; that's what it is in the best cases, and some examples are wonderfully clever.

Florentia. Then what fault do you find? Dorriforth. Simply this—that the whole is a pictorial whole, not a dramatic one. There is something indeed that you can't pick out, for the very good reason that—in any serious sense of the word—it isn't there.

Florentia. The public has taste, then, if it recognizes and delights in a fine picture.

Dorriforth. I never said it hadn't, so far as that goes. The public likes to be amused, and small blame to it. It isn't very particular about the means, but it has rather a preference for amusements that I believes to be "improving," other things being equal. I don't think it's either very intelligent or at all opinionated, the dear old public it takes humbly enough what is given it and it doesn't cry for the moon. It has an idea that fine scenery is an appeal to its nobler part, and that it shows a nice critical sense in preferring it to poor. That's a real intellectual flight, for the public.

Auberon. Very well, its preference is right, and why isn't that a perfectly legitimate state of things?

Dorriforth. Why isn't it? It distinctly *is!* Good scenery and poor acting are better than poor scenery with the same sauce. Only it becomes then another matter: we are no longer talking about the drama.

Auberon. Very likely that's the future of the drama, in London—an immense elaboration of the picture.

Dorriforth. My dear fellow, you take the words out of my mouth. An immense elaboration of the picture and an immense sacrifice of everything else: it would take very little more to persuade me that that will be the only formula for our children. It's all right, when once we have buried our dead. I have no doubt that the scenic part of the art, remarkable as some of its achievements already appear to us, is only in its infancy, and that we are destined to see wonders done that we now but faintly conceive. The probable extension of the mechanical arts is infinite. "Built in," forsooth! We shall see castles and cities and mountains and rivers built in. Everything points that way; especially the constitution of the contemporary multitude. It is huge and good-natured and common. It likes big, unmistakable, knock-down effects; it likes to get its money back in palpable, computable change. It's in a tremendous hurry, squeezed together, with a sort of generalized gape, and the last thing it expects of you is that you will spin things fine. You can't portray a character, alas, or even, vividly, any sort of human figure, unless, in some degree, you do that. Therefore the theatre, inevitably accommodating itself, will be at last a landscape without figures. I mean, of course, without figures that count. There will be little illustrations of costume stuck about—dressed manikins; but they'll have nothing to say: they won't even go through the form of speech.

Amicia. What a hideous prospect!

Dorriforth. Not necessarily, for we shall have grown used to it: we shall, as I say, have buried our dead. To-day it's cruel, because our old ideals are only dying, they are *in extremis*, they are virtually defunct, but they are above-ground—we trip and stumble on them. We shall eventually lay them tidily away. This is a bad moment, because it's a moment of transition, and we still *miss* the old superstition, the bravery of execution, the eloquence of the lips, the interpretation of character. We miss these things, of course, in proportion as the ostensible occasion for them is great; we miss them particularly, for instance, when the curtain rises on Shakespeare. Then we are conscious of a certain divine dissatisfaction, of a yearning for that which isn't. But we shall have got over this discomfort on the day when we have accepted the ostensible occasion as merely and frankly ostensible, and the real one as having nothing to do with it.

Florentia. I don't follow you. As I'm one of the squeezed, gaping public, I must be dense and vulgar. You do, by-the-way, immense injustice to that body. They do care for character—care much for it. Aren't they perpetually talking about the actor's conception of it?

Dorriforth. Dear lady, what better proof can there be of their ineptitude, and that painted canvas and real water are the only things they understand? The vanity of wasting time over that!

Auberon. Over what?

Dorriforth. The actor's conception of a part. It's the refuge of observers who are no observers and critics who are no critics. With what on earth have we to do save his execution?

Florentia. I don't in the least agree with you.

Amicia. Are you very sure, my poor Dorriforth?

Auberon. Give him rope and he'll hang himself.

Dorriforth. It doesn't need any great license to ask who in the world holds in his bosom the sacred secret of the right conception. All the actor can do is to give us his. We must take that one for granted, we make him a present of it. He must impose his conception upon us—

Auberon (interrupting). I thought you said we accepted it.

Dorriforth. Impose it upon our *attention*. clever Auberon. It is because we accept his idea that he must repay us by making it vivid, by showing us how valuable it is. We give him a watch: he must show us what time it keeps. He winds it up, that is he executes the conception, and his execution is what we criticise, if we be so moved. Can anything be more absurd than to hear people discussing the conception of a part of which the execution doesn't exist—the idea of a character which never arrives at form? Think what it is, that form, as an accomplished actor may give it to us, and admit that we have enough to do to hold him to this particular honor.

Auberon. Do you mean to say you don't think some conceptions are better than some others?

Dorriforth. Most assuredly, some are better: the proof of the pudding is in the eating. The best are those which yield the most points, which have the largest face; those, in other words, that are the most demonstrable, or, in other words still, the most actable. The most intelligent performer is he who recognizes most surely this "actable" and distinguishes in it the more from the less. But we are so far from being in possession of a subjective pattern to which we have a right to hold him that he is entitled directly to contradict any such absolute by presenting us with different versions of the same text, each completely colored, completely consistent with itself. Every actor in whom the artistic life is strong must often feel the challenge to do that. I should never think, for instance, of contesting an actress's right to represent Lady Macbeth as a charming, insinuating woman, if she really sees the figure that way. I may be surprised at such a vision; but so far from being scandalized, I am positively thankful for the extension of knowledge, of pleasure, that she is able to open to me.

Auberon. A reading, as they say, either commends itself to one's sense of truth or it doesn't. In the one case—

Dorriforth. In the one case I recognize—even—or especially—when the presumption may have been against the particular attempt, a consummate illustration of what art can do. In the other I moralize indulgently upon human rashness.

Florentia. You have an assurance *à taute épreuve*; but you are deplorably superficial. There is a whole group of plays and a whole category of acting to which your generalizations quite fail to apply. Help me, Auberon.

Auberon. You're easily exhausted. I suppose she means that it's far from true everywhere that the scenery is everything. It may be true—I don't say it is!—of two or three good-natured playhouses in London. It isn't true—how can it be?—of the provincial theatres or of the others in the capital. Put it even that they would be all scenery if they could; they can't, poor things—so they have to provide acting.

Dorriforth. They have to, fortunately; but what do we hear of it?

Florentia. How do you mean, what do we hear of it?

Dorriforth. In what trumpet of fame does it reach us? They do what they can, the performers Auberon alludes to, and they are brave souls. But I am speaking of the conspicuous cases, of the exhibitions that draw.

Florentia. There is good acting that draws; one could give you names and places.

Dorriforth. I have already guessed those you mean. But when it isn't too much a matter of the paraphernalia it is too little a matter of the play. A play nowadays is a rare bird. I should like to see ¦ one. **Florentia.** There are lots of them, all the while—the newspapers talk about them. People talk about them at dinners.

Dorriforth. What do they say about them?

Florentia. The newspapers?

Dorriforth. No, I don't care for *them*. The people at dinners.

Florentia. Oh. they don't say anything in particular.

Dorriforth. Doesn't that seem to show the effort isn't very suggestive?

Amicia. The conversation at dinners certainly isn't.

Dorriforth. I mean our contemporary drama. To begin with, you can't find it there's no text.

Florentia. No text?

Auberon. So much the better!

Dorriforth. So much the better if there is to be no criticism. There is only a dirt prompter's book. One can't put one's hand upon it; one doesn't know what one is discussing. There is no "authority"—nothing is ever published.

Amicia. The pieces wouldn't bear that.

Dorriforth. It would be a small ordeal to resist—if there were anything in them. Look at the novels!

Amicia. The text is the French *brochure*. The "adaptation" is unprintable.

Dorriforth. That's where it's so wrong, It ought at least to be as good as the original.

Auberon. Aren't there some "rights" to protect—some risk of the play being stolen if it's published?

Dorriforth. There may be—I don't know. Doesn't that only prove how little important we regard the drama as being, and how little seriously we take it, if we won't even trouble ourselves to bring about decent civil conditions for its existence? What have we to do with the French *brochure?* how does that help us to represent our own life, our manners, our customs, our ideas, our English types, our English world? Such a field for comedy, for tragedy, for portraiture, for satire, as they all make-such subjects as they would yield! Think of London alone—what a matchless hunting-ground for the satirist— the most magnificent that ever was. If the occasion always produced the man London would have produced an Aristophanes. But somehow it doesn't.

Florentia. Oh, types and ideas, Aristophanes and satire—!

Dorriforth. I'm too ambitious, you mean? I shall presently show you that I'm not ambitious at all. Everything makes against that—I am only reading the signs.

Auberon. The plays are arranged to be as English as possible: they are altered, they are fitted.

Dorriforth. Fitted? Indeed they are, and to the capacity of infants. They are in too many cases made vulgar, puerile, barbarous. They are neither fish nor flesh, and with all the point that's left out and all the naïveté that's put in, they cease to place before us any coherent appeal or any recognizable society.

Auberon. They often make good plays to act, all the same.

Dorriforth. They may; but they don't make good plays to see or to hear. The theatre consists of two things, *que diable*—of the stage and the drama, and I don't see how you can have it unless you have both, or how you can have either unless you have the other. They are the two blades of a pair of scissors.

Auberon. You are very unfair to native talent. There are lots of *strictly original* plays—

Amicia. Yes, they put that expression on the posters.

Auberon. I don't know what they put on the posters; but the plays are written and acted—produced with great success.

Dorriforth. Produced—partly. A play isn't fully produced until it is in a form in which you can refer to it. We have to talk in the air. I can refer to my Congreve, but I can't to my Pinero. {*}

* Since the above was written several of Mr. Pinero's plays have been published.

Florentia. The authors are not bound to publish them if they don't wish.

Dorriforth. Certainly not, nor are they in that case bound to insist on one's not being a little vague about them. They are perfectly free to withhold them; they may have very good reasons for it, and I can imagine some that would be excellent and worthy of all respect. But their withholding them is one of the signs.

Auberon. What signs?

Dorriforth. Those I just spoke of—those we are trying to read together. The signs that ambition and desire are folly, that the sun of the drama has set, that the matter isn't worth talking about, that it has ceased to be an interest for serious folk, and that everything—everything, I mean, that's anything—is over. The sooner we recognize it the sooner to sleep, the sooner we get clear of misleading illusions and are purged of the bad blood that disappointment makes. It's a pity, because the theatre—after every allowance is made— *might* have been a fine thing. At all events it was a pleasant—it was really almost a noble—dream. *Requiescat!*

Florentia. I see nothing to confirm your absurd theory. I delight in the play; more people than ever delight in it with me; more people than ever go to it, and there are ten theatres in London where there were two of old.

Dorriforth. Which is what was to demonstrated. Whence do they derive their nutriment?

Auberon. Why, from the enormous public.

Dorriforth. My dear fellow, I'm not talking of the box-office. What wealth of dramatic, of histrionic production have we to meet that enormous demand? There will be twenty theatres ten years hence where there are ten to-day, and there will be, no doubt, ten times as many people "delighting in them," like Florentla. But it won't alter the fact that our dream will have been dreamed. Florentia said a word when we came in which alone speaks volumes.

Florentia. What was my word?

Auberon. You are sovereignly unjust to native talent among the actors—I leave the dramatists alone. There are many who do excellent, independent work; strive for perfection, completeness—in short, the things we want.

Dorriforth. I am not in the least unjust to them—I only pity them: they have so little to put *sous la dent*. It must seem to them at times that no one will work for them, that they are likely to starve for parts—forsaken of gods and men.

Florentia. If they work, then, in solitude and sadness, they have the more honor, and one should recognize more explicitly their great merit.

Dorriforth. Admirably said. Their laudable effort is precisely the one little loop-hole that I see of escape from the general doom. Certainly we must try to enlarge it—that small aperture into the blue. We must fix our eyes on it and make much of it, exaggerate it, do anything with it that may contribute to restore a working faith. Precious that must be to the sincere spirits on the stage who are conscious of all the other things—formidable things—that rise against them.

Amicia. What other things do you mean?

Dorriforth. Why, for one thing, the grossness and brutality of London, with its scramble, its pressure, its hustle of engagements, of preoccupations, its long distances, its late hours, its nightly dinners, its innumerable demands on the attention, its general congregation of influences fatal to the isolation, to the punctuality, to the security, of the dear old playhouse spell. When Florentia said in her charming way—

Florentia. Here's my dreadful speech at last.

Dorriforth. When you said that you went to the Théâtre Libre in the afternoon because you couldn't spare an evening, I recognized the death-knell of the drama. *Time*, the very breath of its nostrils, is lacking. Wagner was clever to go to leisurely Bayreuth among the hills—the Bayreuth of spacious days, a paradise of "development."

Talk to a London audience of "development!" The long runs would, if necessary, put the whole question into a nutshell. Figure to yourself, for then the question is answered, how an intelligent actor must loathe them, and what a cruel negation he must find in them of the artistic life, the life of which the very essence is variety of practice, freshness of experiment, and to feel that one must do many things in turn to do any one of them completely.

Auberon. I don't in the least understand your *acharnement*, in view of the vagueness of your contention.

Dorriforth. My *acharnement* is your little joke, and my contention is a little lesson in philosophy.

Florentia. I prefer a lesson in taste. I had one the other night at the "Merry Wives."

Dorriforth. If you come to that, so did I!

Amicia. So she does spare an evening sometimes.

Florentia. It was all extremely quiet and comfortable, and I don't in the least recognize Dorriforth's lurid picture of the dreadful conditions. There was no scenery—at least not too much; there was just enough, and it was very pretty, and it was in its place.

Dorriforth. And what else was there?

Florentia. There was very good acting.

Amicia. I also went, and I thought it all, for a sportive, wanton thing, quite painfully ugly.

Auberon. Uglier than that ridiculous black room, with the invisible people groping about in it, of your precious "Duc d'Enghien?"

Dorriforth. The black room is doubtless not the last word of art, but it struck me as a successful application of a happy idea. The contrivance was perfectly simple—a closer night effect than is usually attempted, with a few guttering candles, which threw high shadows over the bare walls, on the table of the court-martial. Out of the gloom came the voices and tones of the distinguishable figures, and it is perhaps a fancy of mine that it made them—given the situation, of course—more impressive and dramatic.

Auberon. You rail against scenery, but what could belong more to the order of things extraneous to what you perhaps a little priggishly call the delicacy of personal art than the arrangement you are speaking of?

Dorriforth. I was talking of the abuse of scenery. I never said anything so idiotic as that the effect isn't helped by an appeal to the eye and an adumbration of the whereabouts.

Auberon. But where do you draw the line and fix the limit? What is the exact dose?

Dorriforth. It's a question of taste and tact.

Florentia. And did you find taste and tact in that coal-hole of the Théâtre Libre?

Dorriforth. Coal-hole is again your joke. I found a strong impression in it—an impression of the hurried, extemporized cross-examination, by night, of an impatient and mystified prisoner, whose dreadful fate had been determined in advance, who was to be shot, high-handedly, in the dismal dawn. The arrangement didn't worry and distract me: it was simplifying, intensifying. It gave, what a judicious *mise-en-scène* should always do, the essence of the matter, and left the embroidery to the actors.

Florentia. At the "Merry Wives," where you could see your hand before your face, I could make out the embroidery.

Dorriforth. Could you, under Falstaff's pasteboard cheeks and the sad disfigurement of his mates? There was no excess of scenery, Auberon says. Why, Falstaff's very person was nothing *but* scenery. A false face, a false figure, false hands, false legs—scarcely a square inch on which the irrepressible humor of the rogue could break into illustrative touches. And he is so human, so expressive, of so rich a physiognomy. One would rather Mr. Beerbohm Tree should have played the part in his own clever, elegant slimness—that would at least have represented life. A Falstaff all "make-up" is an opaque substance.

This seems to me an example of what the rest still more suggested, that in dealing with a production like the "Merry Wives" really the main quality to put forward is discretion. You must resolve such a production, as a thing represented, into a tone that the imagination can take an aesthetic pleasure in. Its grossness must be transposed, as it were, to a fictive scale, a scale of fainter tints and generalized signs. A filthy, eruptive, realistic Bardolph and Pistol overlay the romantic with the literal. Relegate them and blur them, to the eye; let their blotches be constructive and their raggedness relative.

Amicia. Ah, it was *so* ugly!

Dorriforth. What a pity then, after all, there wasn't more painted canvas to divert you! Ah, decidedly, the theatre of the future must be that.

Florentia. Please remember your theory that our life's a scramble, and suffer me to go and dress for dinner.

1889.

About Author

Henry James OM (15 April 1843 – 28 February 1916) was an American-British author regarded as a key transitional figure between literary realism and literary modernism, and is considered by many to be among the greatest novelists in the English language. He was the son of Henry James Sr. and the brother of renowned philosopher and psychologist William James and diarist Alice James.

He is best known for a number of novels dealing with the social and marital interplay between émigré Americans, English people, and continental Europeans. Examples of such novels include The Portrait of a Lady, The Ambassadors, and The Wings of the Dove. His later works were increasingly experimental. In describing the internal states of mind and social dynamics of his characters, James often made use of a style in which ambiguous or contradictory motives and impressions were overlaid or juxtaposed in the discussion of a character's psyche. For their unique ambiguity, as well as for other aspects of their composition, his late works have been compared to impressionist painting.

His novella The Turn of the Screw has garnered a reputation as the most analysed and ambiguous ghost story in the English language and remains his most widely adapted work in other media. He also wrote a number of other highly regarded ghost stories and is considered one of the greatest masters of the field.

James published articles and books of criticism, travel, biography, autobiography, and plays. Born in the United States, James largely relocated to Europe as a young man and eventually settled in England, becoming a British subject in 1915, one year before his death. James was nominated for the Nobel Prize in Literature in 1911, 1912 and 1916.

Life

Early years, 1843–1883

James was born at 2 Washington Place in New York City on 15 April 1843. His parents were Mary Walsh and Henry James Sr. His father was intelligent and steadfastly congenial. He was a lecturer and philosopher who had inherited independent means from his father, an Albany banker and investor. Mary came from a wealthy family long settled in New York City. Her sister Katherine lived with her adult family for an extended period of time. Henry Jr. had three brothers, William, who was one year his senior, and younger brothers Wilkinson (Wilkie) and Robertson. His younger sister was Alice. Both of his parents were of Irish and Scottish descent.

The family first lived in Albany, at 70 N. Pearl St., and then moved to Fourteenth Street in New York City when James was still a young boy. His education was calculated by his father to expose him to many influences, primarily scientific and philosophical; it was described by Percy Lubbock, the editor of his selected letters, as "extraordinarily haphazard and promiscuous." James did not share the usual education in Latin and Greek classics. Between 1855 and 1860, the James' household traveled to London, Paris, Geneva, Boulogne-sur-Mer and Newport, Rhode Island, according to the father's current interests and publishing ventures, retreating to the United States when funds were low. Henry studied primarily with tutors and briefly attended schools while the family traveled in Europe. Their longest stays were in France, where Henry began to feel at home and became fluent in French. He was afflicted with a stutter, which seems to have manifested itself only when he spoke English; in French, he did not stutter.

In 1860 the family returned to Newport. There Henry became a friend of the painter John La Farge, who introduced him to French literature, and in particular, to Balzac. James later called Balzac his "greatest master," and said that he had learned more about the craft of fiction from him than from anyone else.

In the autumn of 1861 Henry received an injury, probably to his back, while fighting a fire. This injury, which resurfaced at times throughout his life, made him unfit for military service in the American Civil War.

In 1864 the James family moved to Boston, Massachusetts to be near William, who had enrolled first in the Lawrence Scientific School at Harvard and then in the medical school. In 1862 Henry attended Harvard Law School, but realised that he was not interested in studying law. He pursued his interest in literature and associated with authors and critics William Dean Howells and Charles Eliot Norton in Boston and Cambridge, formed lifelong friendships with Oliver Wendell Holmes Jr., the future Supreme Court Justice, and with James and Annie Fields, his first professional mentors.

His first published work was a review of a stage performance, "Miss Maggie Mitchell in Fanchon the Cricket," published in 1863. About a year later, A Tragedy of Error, his first short story, was published anonymously. James's first payment was for an appreciation of Sir Walter Scott's novels, written for the North American Review. He wrote fiction and non-fiction pieces for The Nation and Atlantic Monthly, where Fields was editor. In 1871 he published his first novel, Watch and Ward, in serial form in the Atlantic Monthly. The novel was later published in book form in 1878.

During a 14-month trip through Europe in 1869–70 he met Ruskin, Dickens, Matthew Arnold, William Morris, and George Eliot. Rome impressed him profoundly. "Here I am then in the Eternal City," he wrote to his brother William. "At last—for the first time—I live!" He attempted to support himself as a freelance writer in Rome, then secured a position as Paris correspondent for the New York Tribune, through the influence of its editor John Hay. When these efforts failed he returned to New York City. During 1874 and 1875 he published Transatlantic Sketches, A Passionate Pilgrim, and Roderick Hudson. During this early period in his career he was influenced by Nathaniel Hawthorne.

In 1869 he settled in London. There he established relationships with Macmillan and other publishers, who paid for serial installments that they would later publish in book form. The audience for these serialized novels was largely made up of middle-class women, and James struggled to fashion serious literary work within the strictures imposed by editors' and publishers' notions of what was suitable for young women to read. He lived in rented rooms but was able to join gentlemen's clubs that had libraries and where he could entertain male friends. He was introduced to English society by Henry Adams and Charles Milnes Gaskell, the latter introducing him to the Travellers' and the Reform Clubs.

In the fall of 1875 he moved to the Latin Quarter of Paris. Aside from two trips to America, he spent the next three decades—the rest of his life—in Europe. In Paris he met Zola, Alphonse Daudet, Maupassant, Turgenev, and others. He stayed in Paris only a year before moving to London.

In England he met the leading figures of politics and culture. He continued to be a prolific writer, producing The American (1877), The Europeans (1878), a revision of Watch and Ward (1878), French Poets and Novelists (1878), Hawthorne (1879), and several shorter works of fiction. In 1878 Daisy Miller established his fame on both sides of the Atlantic. It drew notice perhaps mostly because it depicted a woman whose behavior is outside the social norms of Europe. He also began his first masterpiece, The Portrait of a Lady, which would appear in 1881.

In 1877 he first visited Wenlock Abbey in Shropshire, home of his friend Charles Milnes Gaskell whom he had met through Henry Adams. He was much inspired by the darkly romantic Abbey and the surrounding countryside, which features in his essay Abbeys and Castles. In particular the gloomy monastic fishponds behind the Abbey are said to have inspired the lake in The Turn of the Screw.

While living in London, James continued to follow the careers of the "French realists", Émile Zola in particular. Their stylistic methods influenced his own work in the years to come. Hawthorne's influence on him faded during this period, replaced by George Eliot and Ivan Turgenev. 1879–1882 saw the publication of The Europeans, Washington Square, Confidence, and The Portrait of a Lady. He visited America in 1882–1883, then returned to London.

The period from 1881 to 1883 was marked by several losses. His mother died in 1881, followed by his father a few months later, and then by his brother Wilkie. Emerson, an old family friend, died in 1882. His friend Turgenev died in 1883.

Middle years, 1884–1897

In 1884 James made another visit to Paris. There he met again with Zola, Daudet, and Goncourt. He had been following the careers of the French "realist" or "naturalist" writers, and was increasingly influenced by them. In 1886, he published The Bostonians and The Princess Casamassima, both influenced by the French writers he'd studied assiduously. Critical reaction and sales were poor. He wrote to Howells that the books had hurt his career rather than helped because they had "reduced the desire, and demand, for my productions to zero". During this time he became friends with Robert Louis Stevenson, John Singer Sargent, Edmund Gosse, George du Maurier, Paul Bourget, and Constance Fenimore Woolson. His third novel from the 1880s was The Tragic Muse. Although he was following the precepts of Zola in his novels of the '80s, their tone and attitude are closer to the fiction of Alphonse Daudet. The lack of critical and financial success for his novels during this period led him to try writing for the theatre. (His dramatic works and his experiences with theatre are discussed below.)

In the last quarter of 1889, he started translating "for pure and copious lucre" Port Tarascon, the third volume of Alphonse Daudet adventures of Tartarin de Tarascon. Serialized in Harper's Monthly Magazine from June 1890, this translation praised as "clever" by The Spectator was published in January 1891 by Sampson Low, Marston, Searle & Rivington.

After the stage failure of Guy Domville in 1895, James was near despair and thoughts of death plagued him. The years spent on dramatic works were not entirely a loss. As he moved into the last phase of his career he found ways to adapt dramatic techniques into the novel form.

In the late 1880s and throughout the 1890s James made several trips through Europe. He spent a long stay in Italy in 1887. In that year the short novel The Aspern Papers and The Reverberator were published.

Late years, 1898–1916

In 1897–1898 he moved to Rye, Sussex, and wrote The Turn of the Screw. 1899–1900 saw the publication of The Awkward Age and The Sacred

Fount. During 1902–1904 he wrote The Ambassadors, The Wings of the Dove, and The Golden Bowl.

In 1904 he revisited America and lectured on Balzac. In 1906–1910 he published The American Scene and edited the "New York Edition", a 24-volume collection of his works. In 1910 his brother William died; Henry had just joined William from an unsuccessful search for relief in Europe on what then turned out to be his (Henry's) last visit to the United States (from summer 1910 to July 1911), and was near him, according to a letter he wrote, when he died.

In 1913 he wrote his autobiographies, A Small Boy and Others, and Notes of a Son and Brother. After the outbreak of the First World War in 1914 he did war work. In 1915 he became a British subject and was awarded the Order of Merit the following year. He died on 28 February 1916, in Chelsea, London. As he requested, his ashes were buried in Cambridge Cemetery in Massachusetts.

Biographers

James regularly rejected suggestions that he should marry, and after settling in London proclaimed himself "a bachelor". F. W. Dupee, in several volumes on the James family, originated the theory that he had been in love with his cousin Mary ("Minnie") Temple, but that a neurotic fear of sex kept him from admitting such affections: "James's invalidism ... was itself the symptom of some fear of or scruple against sexual love on his part." Dupee used an episode from James's memoir A Small Boy and Others, recounting a dream of a Napoleonic image in the Louvre, to exemplify James's romanticism about Europe, a Napoleonic fantasy into which he fled.

Dupee had not had access to the James family papers and worked principally from James's published memoir of his older brother, William, and the limited collection of letters edited by Percy Lubbock, heavily weighted toward James's last years. His account therefore moved directly from James's childhood, when he trailed after his older brother, to elderly invalidism. As more material became available to scholars, including the diaries of contemporaries and hundreds of affectionate and sometimes erotic letters written by James to younger men, the picture of neurotic celibacy gave way to a portrait of a closeted homosexual.

Between 1953 and 1972, Leon Edel authored a major five-volume biography of James, which accessed unpublished letters and documents after Edel gained the permission of James's family. Edel's portrayal of James included the suggestion he was celibate. It was a view first propounded by critic Saul Rosenzweig in 1943. In 1996 Sheldon M. Novick published Henry James: The Young Master, followed by Henry James: The Mature Master (2007). The first book "caused something of an uproar in Jamesian circles" as it challenged the previous received notion of celibacy, a once-familiar paradigm in biographies of homosexuals when direct evidence was non-existent. Novick also criticised Edel for following the discounted Freudian interpretation of homosexuality "as a kind of failure." The difference of opinion erupted in a series of exchanges between Edel and Novick which were published by the online magazine Slate, with the latter arguing that even the suggestion of celibacy went against James's own injunction "live!"—not "fantasize!"

A letter James wrote in old age to Hugh Walpole has been cited as an explicit statement of this. Walpole confessed to him of indulging in "high jinks", and James wrote a reply endorsing it: "We must know, as much as possible, in our beautiful art, yours & mine, what we are talking about — & the only way to know it is to have lived & loved & cursed & floundered & enjoyed & suffered — I don't think I regret a single 'excess' of my responsive youth".

The interpretation of James as living a less austere emotional life has been subsequently explored by other scholars. The often intense politics of Jamesian scholarship has also been the subject of studies. Author Colm Tóibín has said that Eve Kosofsky Sedgwick's Epistemology of the Closet made a landmark difference to Jamesian scholarship by arguing that he be read as a homosexual writer whose desire to keep his sexuality a secret shaped his layered style and dramatic artistry. According to Tóibín such a reading "removed James from the realm of dead white males who wrote about posh people. He became our contemporary."

James's letters to expatriate American sculptor Hendrik Christian Andersen have attracted particular attention. James met the 27-year-old Andersen in Rome in 1899, when James was 56, and wrote letters to Andersen that are intensely emotional: "I hold you, dearest boy, in my innermost love, & count on your feeling me—in every throb of your soul". In a letter of 6 May 1904, to his brother William, James referred to himself as "always your hopelessly celibate even though sexagenarian Henry". How accurate that description might have been is the subject of contention among James's biographers,   but the letters to Andersen were occasionally quasi-erotic: "I put, my dear boy, my arm around you, & feel the pulsation, thereby, as it were, of our excellent future & your admirable endowment." To his homosexual friend Howard Sturgis, James could write: "I repeat, almost to indiscretion, that I could live with you. Meanwhile I can only try to live without you."

His numerous letters to the many young gay men among his close male friends are more forthcoming. In a letter to Howard Sturgis, following a long visit, James refers jocularly to their "happy little congress of two" and in letters to Hugh Walpole he pursues convoluted jokes and puns about their relationship, referring to himself as an elephant who "paws you oh so benevolently" and winds about Walpole his "well meaning old trunk". His letters to Walter Berry printed by the Black Sun Press have long been celebrated for their lightly veiled eroticism.

He corresponded in almost equally extravagant language with his many female friends, writing, for example, to fellow novelist Lucy Clifford: "Dearest Lucy! What shall I say? when I love you so very, very much, and see you nine times for once that I see Others! Therefore I think that—if you want it made clear to the meanest intelligence—I love you more than I love Others." To his New York friend Mary Cadwalader Jones: "Dearest Mary Cadwalader. I yearn over you, but I yearn in vain; & your long silence really breaks my heart, mystifies, depresses, almost alarms me, to the point even of making me wonder if poor unconscious & doting old Célimare [Jones's pet name for James] has 'done' anything, in some dark somnambulism of the spirit, which has ... given you a bad moment, or a wrong impression, or a 'colourable pretext' ... However these things may be, he loves you as tenderly as ever;

nothing, to the end of time, will ever detach him from you, & he remembers those Eleventh St. matutinal intimes hours, those telephonic matinées, as the most romantic of his life ..." His long friendship with American novelist Constance Fenimore Woolson, in whose house he lived for a number of weeks in Italy in 1887, and his shock and grief over her suicide in 1894, are discussed in detail in Edel's biography and play a central role in a study by Lyndall Gordon. (Edel conjectured that Woolson was in love with James and killed herself in part because of his coldness, but Woolson's biographers have objected to Edel's account.)

Works

Style and themes

James is one of the major figures of trans-Atlantic literature. His works frequently juxtapose characters from the Old World (Europe), embodying a feudal civilisation that is beautiful, often corrupt, and alluring, and from the New World (United States), where people are often brash, open, and assertive and embody the virtues—freedom and a more highly evolved moral character—of the new American society. James explores this clash of personalities and cultures, in stories of personal relationships in which power is exercised well or badly. His protagonists were often young American women facing oppression or abuse, and as his secretary Theodora Bosanquet remarked in her monograph Henry James at Work:

> When he walked out of the refuge of his study and into the world and looked around him, he saw a place of torment, where creatures of prey perpetually thrust their claws into the quivering flesh of doomed, defenseless children of light ... His novels are a repeated exposure of this wickedness, a reiterated and passionate plea for the fullest freedom of development, unimperiled by reckless and barbarous stupidity.

Critics have jokingly described three phases in the development of James's prose: "James I, James II, and The Old Pretender." He wrote short stories and plays. Finally, in his third and last period he returned to the long, serialised novel. Beginning in the second period, but most noticeably in the third, he increasingly abandoned direct statement in favour of frequent double negatives, and complex descriptive imagery. Single paragraphs began to run for page after page, in which an initial noun would be succeeded by pronouns surrounded by clouds of adjectives and prepositional clauses, far from their original referents, and verbs would be deferred and then preceded by a series of adverbs. The overall effect could be a vivid evocation of a scene as perceived by a sensitive observer. It has been debated whether this change of style was engendered by James's shifting from writing to dictating to a typist, a change made during the composition of What Maisie Knew.

In its intense focus on the consciousness of his major characters, James's later work foreshadows extensive developments in 20th century fiction. Indeed, he might have influenced stream-of-consciousness writers such as Virginia Woolf, who not only read some of his novels but also wrote essays about them. Both contemporary and modern readers have found the late style difficult and unnecessary; his friend Edith Wharton, who admired him greatly, said that there were passages in his work that were all but incomprehensible. James was harshly portrayed by H. G. Wells as a hippopotamus laboriously attempting to pick up a pea that had got into a corner of its cage. The "late James" style was ably parodied by Max Beerbohm in "The Mote in the Middle Distance".

More important for his work overall may have been his position as an expatriate, and in other ways an outsider, living in Europe. While he came from middle-class and provincial beginnings (seen from the perspective of European polite society) he worked very hard to gain access to all levels of society, and the settings of his fiction range from working class to aristocratic, and often describe the efforts of middle-class Americans to make their way in European capitals. He confessed he got some of his best story ideas from gossip at the dinner table or at country house weekends. He worked for a living, however, and lacked the experiences of select schools, university, and army service, the common bonds of masculine society. He was furthermore a man whose tastes and interests were, according to the prevailing standards of Victorian era Anglo-American culture, rather feminine, and who was shadowed by the cloud of prejudice that then and later accompanied suspicions of his homosexuality. Edmund Wilson famously compared James's objectivity to Shakespeare's:

One would be in a position to appreciate James better if one compared him with the dramatists of the seventeenth century—Racine and Molière, whom he resembles in form as well as in point of view, and even Shakespeare, when allowances are made for the most extreme differences in subject and form. These poets are not, like Dickens and Hardy, writers of melodrama—either humorous or pessimistic, nor secretaries of society like Balzac, nor prophets like Tolstoy: they are occupied simply with the presentation of conflicts of moral character, which they do not concern themselves about softening or averting. They do not indict society for these situations: they regard them as universal and inevitable. They do not even blame God for allowing them: they accept them as the conditions of life.

It is also possible to see many of James's stories as psychological thought-experiments. In his preface to the New York edition of The American he describes the development of the story in his mind as exactly such: the "situation" of an American, "some robust but insidiously beguiled and betrayed, some cruelly wronged, compatriot..." with the focus of the story being on the response of this wronged man. The Portrait of a Lady may be an experiment to see what happens when an idealistic young woman suddenly becomes very rich. In many of his tales, characters seem to exemplify alternative futures and possibilities, as most markedly in "The Jolly Corner", in which the protagonist and a ghost-doppelganger live alternative American and European lives; and in others, like The Ambassadors, an older James seems fondly to regard his own younger self facing a crucial moment.

Major novels

The first period of James's fiction, usually considered to have culminated in The Portrait of a Lady, concentrated on the contrast between Europe and America. The style of these novels is generally straightforward and, though personally characteristic, well within the norms of 19th-century fiction. Roderick Hudson (1875) is a Künstlerroman that traces the development of the title character, an extremely talented sculptor. Although the book shows some signs of immaturity—this was James's first serious attempt at a full-length novel—it has attracted favourable comment due to the vivid realisation of the three major characters: Roderick Hudson, superbly gifted but unstable and unreliable; Rowland Mallet, Roderick's limited but much more mature friend and patron; and Christina Light, one of James's most enchanting and maddening femmes fatales. The pair of Hudson and Mallet has been seen as representing the two sides of James's own nature: the wildly imaginative artist and the brooding conscientious mentor.

In The Portrait of a Lady (1881) James concluded the first phase of his career with a novel that remains his most popular piece of long fiction. The story is of a spirited young American woman, Isabel Archer, who "affronts her destiny" and finds it overwhelming. She inherits a large amount of money and subsequently becomes the victim of Machiavellian scheming by two American expatriates. The narrative is set mainly in Europe, especially in England and Italy. Generally regarded as the masterpiece of his early phase, The Portrait of a Lady is described as a psychological novel, exploring the minds of his characters, and almost a work of social science, exploring the differences between Europeans and Americans, the old and the new worlds.

The second period of James's career, which extends from the publication of The Portrait of a Lady through the end of the nineteenth century, features less popular novels including The Princess Casamassima, published serially in The Atlantic Monthly in 1885–1886, and The Bostonians, published serially in The Century Magazine during the same period. This period also featured James's celebrated Gothic novella, The Turn of the Screw.

The third period of James's career reached its most significant achievement in three novels published just around the start of the 20th century: The Wings of the Dove (1902), The Ambassadors (1903), and The Golden Bowl (1904). Critic F. O. Matthiessen called this "trilogy" James's major phase, and these novels have certainly received intense critical study. It was the second-written of the books, The Wings of the Dove (1902) that was the first published because it attracted no serialization. This novel tells the story of Milly Theale, an American heiress stricken with a serious disease, and her impact on the people around her. Some of these people befriend Milly with honourable motives, while others are more self-interested. James stated in his autobiographical books that Milly was based on Minny Temple, his beloved cousin who died at an early age of tuberculosis. He said that he attempted in the novel to wrap her memory in the "beauty and dignity of art".

Shorter narratives

James was particularly interested in what he called the "beautiful and blest nouvelle", or the longer form of short narrative. Still, he produced a number of very short stories in which he achieved notable compression of sometimes complex subjects. The following narratives are representative of James's achievement in the shorter forms of fiction.

- "A Tragedy of Error" (1864), short story
- "The Story of a Year" (1865), short story
- A Passionate Pilgrim (1871), novella
- Madame de Mauves (1874), novella
- Daisy Miller (1878), novella
- The Aspern Papers (1888), novella
- The Lesson of the Master (1888), novella
- The Pupil (1891), short story
- "The Figure in the Carpet" (1896), short story
- The Beast in the Jungle (1903), novella
- An International Episode (1878)
- Picture and Text
- Four Meetings (1885)
- A London Life, and Other Tales (1889)
- The Spoils of Poynton (1896)

- Embarrassments (1896)

- The Two Magics: The Turn of the Screw, Covering End (1898)

- A Little Tour of France (1900)

- The Sacred Fount (1901)

- Views and Reviews (1908)

- The Wings of the Dove, Volume I (1902)

- The Wings of the Dove, Volume II (1909)

- The Finer Grain (1910)

- The Outcry (1911)

- Lady Barbarina: The Siege of London, An International Episode and Other Tales (1922)

- The Birthplace (1922)

Plays

At several points in his career James wrote plays, beginning with one-act plays written for periodicals in 1869 and 1871 and a dramatisation of his popular novella Daisy Miller in 1882. From 1890 to 1892, having received a bequest that freed him from magazine publication, he made a strenuous effort to succeed on the London stage, writing a half-dozen plays of which only one, a dramatisation of his novel The American, was produced. This play was performed for several years by a touring repertory company and had a respectable run in London, but did not earn very much money for James. His other plays written at this time were not produced.

In 1893, however, he responded to a request from actor-manager George Alexander for a serious play for the opening of his renovated St. James's Theatre, and wrote a long drama, Guy Domville, which Alexander produced. There was a noisy uproar on the opening night, 5 January 1895, with hissing from the gallery when James took his bow after the final curtain, and the author was upset. The play received moderately good reviews and had a modest run of four weeks before being taken off to make way for Oscar Wilde's The Importance of Being Earnest, which Alexander thought would have better prospects for the coming season.

After the stresses and disappointment of these efforts James insisted that he would write no more for the theatre, but within weeks had agreed to write a curtain-raiser for Ellen Terry. This became the one-act "Summersoft", which he later rewrote into a short story, "Covering End", and then expanded into a full-length play, The High Bid, which had a brief run in London in 1907, when James made another concerted effort to write for the stage. He wrote three new plays, two of which were in production when the death of Edward VII on 6 May 1910 plunged London into mourning and theatres closed. Discouraged by failing health and the stresses of theatrical work, James did not renew his efforts in the theatre, but recycled his plays as successful novels. The Outcry was a best-seller in the United States when it was published in 1911. During the years 1890–1893 when he was most engaged with the theatre, James wrote a good deal of theatrical criticism and assisted Elizabeth Robins and others in translating and producing Henrik Ibsen for the first time in London.

Leon Edel argued in his psychoanalytic biography that James was traumatised by the opening night uproar that greeted Guy Domville, and that it plunged him into a prolonged depression. The successful later novels, in Edel's view, were the result of a kind of self-analysis, expressed in fiction, which partly freed him from his fears. Other biographers and scholars have not accepted this account, however; the more common view being that of F.O. Matthiessen, who wrote: "Instead of being crushed by the collapse of his hopes [for the theatre]... he felt a resurgence of new energy."

Non-fiction

Beyond his fiction, James was one of the more important literary critics in the history of the novel. In his classic essay The Art of Fiction (1884), he argued against rigid prescriptions on the novelist's choice of subject and method of treatment. He maintained that the widest possible freedom in content and approach would help ensure narrative fiction's continued vitality.

James wrote many valuable critical articles on other novelists; typical is his book-length study of Nathaniel Hawthorne, which has been the subject of critical debate. Richard Brodhead has suggested that the study was emblematic of James's struggle with Hawthorne's influence, and constituted an effort to place the elder writer "at a disadvantage." Gordon Fraser, meanwhile, has suggested that the study was part of a more commercial effort by James to introduce himself to British readers as Hawthorne's natural successor.

When James assembled the New York Edition of his fiction in his final years, he wrote a series of prefaces that subjected his own work to searching, occasionally harsh criticism.

At 22 James wrote The Noble School of Fiction for The Nation's first issue in 1865. He would write, in all, over 200 essays and book, art, and theatre reviews for the magazine.

For most of his life James harboured ambitions for success as a playwright. He converted his novel The American into a play that enjoyed modest returns in the early 1890s. In all he wrote about a dozen plays, most of which went unproduced. His costume drama Guy Domville failed disastrously on its opening night in 1895. James then largely abandoned his efforts to conquer the stage and returned to his fiction. In his Notebooks he maintained that his theatrical experiment benefited his novels and tales by helping him dramatise his characters' thoughts "and emotions. James produced a small but valuable amount of theatrical criticism, including perceptive appreciations of Henrik Ibsen.

With his wide-ranging artistic interests, James occasionally wrote on the visual arts. Perhaps his most valuable contribution was his favourable assessment of fellow expatriate John Singer Sargent, a painter whose critical status has improved markedly in recent decades. James also wrote sometimes charming, sometimes brooding articles about various places he visited and lived in. His most famous books of travel writing include Italian Hours (an example of the charming approach) and The American Scene (most definitely on the brooding side).

James was one of the great letter-writers of any era. More than ten thousand of his personal letters are extant, and over three thousand have been published in a large number of collections. A complete edition of James's letters began publication in 2006, edited by Pierre Walker and Greg Zacharias. As of 2014, eight volumes have been published, covering the period from 1855 to 1880. James's correspondents included celebrated contemporaries like Robert Louis Stevenson, Edith Wharton and Joseph Conrad, along with many others in his wide circle of friends and acquaintances. The letters range from the "mere twaddle of graciousness" to serious discussions of artistic, social and personal issues.

Very late in life James began a series of autobiographical works: A Small Boy and Others, Notes of a Son and Brother, and the unfinished The Middle Years. These books portray the development of a classic observer who was passionately interested in artistic creation but was somewhat reticent about participating fully in the life around him.

Reception

Criticism, biographies and fictional treatments

James's work has remained steadily popular with the limited audience of educated readers to whom he spoke during his lifetime, and has remained firmly in the canon, but, after his death, some American critics, such as Van Wyck Brooks, expressed hostility towards James for his long expatriation and eventual naturalisation as a British subject. Other critics such as E. M. Forster complained about what they saw as James's squeamishness in the treatment of sex and other possibly controversial material, or dismissed his late style as difficult and obscure, relying heavily on extremely long sentences and excessively latinate language. Similarly Oscar Wilde criticised him for writing "fiction as if it were a painful duty". Vernon Parrington, composing a canon of American literature, condemned James for having cut himself off from America. Jorge Luis Borges wrote about him, "Despite the scruples and delicate complexities of James, his work suffers from a major defect: the absence of life." And Virginia Woolf, writing to Lytton Strachey, asked, "Please tell me what you find in Henry James. ... we have his works here, and

I read, and I can't find anything but faintly tinged rose water, urbane and sleek, but vulgar and pale as Walter Lamb. Is there really any sense in it?" The novelist W. Somerset Maugham wrote, "He did not know the English as an Englishman instinctively knows them and so his English characters never to my mind quite ring true," and argued "The great novelists, even in seclusion, have lived life passionately. Henry James was content to observe it from a window." Maugham nevertheless wrote, "The fact remains that those last novels of his, notwithstanding their unreality, make all other novels, except the very best, unreadable." Colm Tóibín observed that James "never really wrote about the English very well. His English characters don't work for me."

Despite these criticisms, James is now valued for his psychological and moral realism, his masterful creation of character, his low-key but playful humour, and his assured command of the language. In his 1983 book, The Novels of Henry James, Edward Wagenknecht offers an assessment that echoes Theodora Bosanquet's:

> "To be completely great," Henry James wrote in an early review, "a work of art must lift up the heart," and his own novels do this to an outstanding degree ... More than sixty years after his death, the great novelist who sometimes professed to have no opinions stands foursquare in the great Christian humanistic and democratic tradition. The men and women who, at the height of World War II, raided the secondhand shops for his out-of-print books knew what they were about. For no writer ever raised a braver banner to which all who love freedom might adhere.

William Dean Howells saw James as a representative of a new realist school of literary art which broke with the English romantic tradition epitomised by the works of Charles Dickens and William Makepeace Thackeray. Howells wrote that realism found "its chief exemplar in Mr. James... A novelist he is not, after the old fashion, or after any fashion but his own." F.R. Leavis championed Henry James as a novelist of "established pre-eminence" in The Great Tradition (1948), asserting that The Portrait of a Lady and The Bostonians were "the two most brilliant novels in the language." James is now prized as a master of point of view who moved literary fiction forward by insisting in showing, not telling, his stories to the reader. (Source: Wikipedia)

NOTABLE WORKS

NOVELS

Watch and Ward (1871)

Roderick Hudson (1875)

The American (1877)

The Europeans (1878)

Confidence (1879)

Washington Square (1880)

The Portrait of a Lady (1881)

The Bostonians (1886)

The Princess Casamassima (1886)

The Reverberator (1888)

The Tragic Muse (1890)

The Other House (1896)

The Spoils of Poynton (1897)

What Maisie Knew (1897)

The Awkward Age (1899)

The Sacred Fount (1901)

The Wings of the Dove (1902)

The Ambassadors (1903)

The Golden Bowl (1904)

The Whole Family (collaborative novel with eleven other authors, 1908)

The Outcry (1911)

The Ivory Tower (unfinished, published posthumously 1917)

The Sense of the Past (unfinished, published posthumously 1917)

SHORT STORIES AND NOVELLAS

A Tragedy of Error (1864)

The Story of a Year (1865)

A Landscape Painter (1866)

A Day of Days (1866)

My Friend Bingham (1867)

Poor Richard (1867)

The Story of a Masterpiece (1868)

A Most Extraordinary Case (1868)

A Problem (1868)

De Grey: A Romance (1868)

Osborne's Revenge (1868)

The Romance of Certain Old Clothes (1868)

A Light Man (1869)

Gabrielle de Bergerac (1869)

Travelling Companions (1870)

A Passionate Pilgrim (1871)

At Isella (1871)

Master Eustace (1871)

Guest's Confession (1872)

The Madonna of the Future (1873)

The Sweetheart of M. Briseux (1873)

The Last of the Valerii (1874)

Madame de Mauves (1874)

Adina (1874)

Professor Fargo (1874)

Eugene Pickering (1874)

Benvolio (1875)

Crawford's Consistency (1876)

The Ghostly Rental (1876)

Four Meetings (1877)

Rose-Agathe (1878, as Théodolinde)

Daisy Miller (1878)

Longstaff's Marriage (1878)

An International Episode (1878)

The Pension Beaurepas (1879)

A Diary of a Man of Fifty (1879)

A Bundle of Letters (1879)

The Point of View (1882)

The Siege of London (1883)

Impressions of a Cousin (1883)

Lady Barberina (1884)

Pandora (1884)

The Author of Beltraffio (1884)

Georgina's Reasons (1884)

A New England Winter (1884)

The Path of Duty (1884)

Mrs. Temperly (1887)

Louisa Pallant (1888)

The Aspern Papers (1888)

The Liar (1888)

The Modern Warning (1888, originally published as The Two Countries)

A London Life (1888)

The Patagonia (1888)

The Lesson of the Master (1888)

The Solution (1888)

The Pupil (1891)

Brooksmith (1891)

The Marriages (1891)

The Chaperon (1891)

Sir Edmund Orme (1891)

Nona Vincent (1892)

The Real Thing (1892)

The Private Life (1892)

Lord Beaupré (1892)

The Visits (1892)

Sir Dominick Ferrand (1892)

Greville Fane (1892)

Collaboration (1892)

Owen Wingrave (1892)

The Wheel of Time (1892)

The Middle Years (1893)

The Death of the Lion (1894)

The Coxon Fund (1894)

The Next Time (1895)

Glasses (1896)

The Altar of the Dead (1895)

The Figure in the Carpet (1896)

The Way It Came (1896, also published as The Friends of the Friends)

The Turn of the Screw (1898)

Covering End (1898)

In the Cage (1898)

John Delavoy (1898)

The Given Case (1898)

Europe (1899)

The Great Condition (1899)

The Real Right Thing (1899)

Paste (1899)

The Great Good Place (1900)

Maud-Evelyn (1900)

Miss Gunton of Poughkeepsie (1900)

The Tree of Knowledge (1900)

The Abasement of the Northmores (1900)

The Third Person (1900)

The Special Type (1900)

The Tone of Time (1900)

Broken Wings (1900)

The Two Faces (1900)

Mrs. Medwin (1901)

The Beldonald Holbein (1901)

The Story in It (1902)

Flickerbridge (1902)

The Birthplace (1903)

The Beast in the Jungle (1903)

The Papers (1903)

Fordham Castle (1904)

Julia Bride (1908)

The Jolly Corner (1908)

The Velvet Glove (1909)

Mora Montravers (1909)

Crapy Cornelia (1909)

The Bench of Desolation (1909)

A Round of Visits (1910)

OTHER

Transatlantic Sketches (1875)

French Poets and Novelists (1878)

Hawthorne (1879)

Portraits of Places (1883)

A Little Tour in France (1884)

Partial Portraits (1888)

Essays in London and Elsewhere (1893)

Picture and Text (1893)

Terminations (1893)

Theatricals (1894)

Theatricals: Second Series (1895)

Guy Domville (1895)

The Soft Side (1900)

William Wetmore Story and His Friends (1903)

The Better Sort (1903)

English Hours (1905)

The Question of our Speech; The Lesson of Balzac. Two Lectures (1905)

The American Scene (1907)

Views and Reviews (1908)

Italian Hours (1909)

A Small Boy and Others (1913)

Notes on Novelists (1914)

Notes of a Son and Brother (1914)

Within the Rim (1918)

Travelling Companions (1919)

Notebooks (various, published posthumously)

The Middle Years (unfinished, published posthumously 1917)

A Most Unholy Trade (1925, published posthumously)

The Art of the Novel : Critical Prefaces (1934)

CPSIA information can be obtained
at www.ICGtesting.com
Printed in the USA
LVHW042304050920
665177LV00006B/785